GRANDMA'S SOUPS & SALADS
WITH BISCUITS & BREADS

by Irene Hrechuk
& Verna Zasada

Front Cover: Cioppino, page 77

GRANDMA'S SOUPS & SALADS WITH BISCUITS & BREADS
by
Irene Hrechuk & Verna Zasada

First Printing – July 2004

Published by Publishing Solutions, a division of PrintWest Communications Ltd.

National Library of Canada Cataloguing in Publication Data

Hrechuk, Irene, 1943 –

    Grandma's soups & salads with biscuits & breads / Irene Hrechuk,
    Verna Zasada; Margo Embury, editor.

  Includes index.
  ISBN 1-897010-02-8

1. Soups. 2. Salads. 3. Breads. I. Zasada, Verna, 1934 – II. Embury, Margo, 1943 –
    III. Title: Grandma's soups and salads with biscuits and breads.

TX757.H73 2004   641.8   C2004-904060-X

Food Photography by
Patricia Holdsworth
Patricia Holdsworth Photography
Regina, Saskatchewan

Formatting and index by
Iona Glabus, Centax Books

Designed, Printed and Produced in Canada by
Centax Books, a Division of PrintWest Communications Ltd.
Publishing Director, Editor, Photo Designer & Food Stylist: Margo Embury
1150 Eighth Avenue, Regina, Saskatchewan, Canada S4R 1C9
(306) 525-2304   FAX: (306) 757-2439
centax@printwest.com   www.centaxbooks.com

TABLE OF CONTENTS

Recipes have been tested in U.S. Standard measurements. Common metric measurements are given as a convenience for those who are more familiar with metric. Recipes have not been tested in metric.

INTRODUCTION

More than 60 new soup recipes and over 20 new salad recipes – this collection of over 100 soups and stews and over 70 salads includes a compilation of the best soup, stew, salad, biscuit and bread recipes from the first three *Grandma's* cookbooks. Delicious variation suggestions effectively double the number of recipes.

Grandma's Touch, Grandma's Best, Grandma's Kitchen and, now, *Grandma's Soups & Salads with Biscuits & Breads* – authors Irene Hrechuk and Verna Zasada celebrate traditional favorites from many countries.

Growing up with the wonderful flavors of Norwegian, British, Ukrainian, Polish and "North American" food, they experienced a rich culinary and cultural heritage. Through sharing recipes with new family members, friends and neighbors, they have expanded their repertoire of treasured recipes to reflect our superb multicultural cuisine.

Whatever our culinary heritage, we all have fond memories of the foods we enjoyed as children. Treasured family recipes were part of every special occasion.

Food and hospitality are an important part of our ethnic and personal culture. As we share the hospitality and culture of new friends and family members, we all expand our culinary palates to include new dishes.

Traditional recipes often vary from family to family. In *Grandma's Soups & Salads*, variations and substitutions are included with many basic recipes. These suggestions make the recipes more versatile and inspire novice cooks to be creative in adapting new recipes.

Remembering grandma's kitchen always conjures up images of comforting aromas and satisfying flavors. Grandmas' kitchens contain memories of some of the best food the world has to offer, from generations of great home cooks. With *Grandma's Soups & Salads* you can prepare your special childhood favorites as grandma used to make them.

SOUPS & STEWS

Chilled and refreshing or hearty and comforting, these soups are easy to prepare and satisfying year round. The stews are substantial – full-bodied meals-in-a-bowl to serve after a day at work or a day of outdoor fun. Serve soups or stews with crusty breads and a tossed salad for family lunches or dinners, or for casual entertaining.

BASIC VEGETABLE STOCK

ECONOMICAL AND FAT-FREE, VEGETABLE STOCKS CAN BE VARIED TO SUIT
YOUR PANTRY AND YOUR TASTES

STOCK MAY INCLUDE:

>outer leaves of cabbage, lettuce OR
>   other greens
>cauliflower, broccoli & celery stalks
>peels from washed carrots & parsnips
>   OR whole carrots & parsnips
>leeks, onions with skin on
>garlic cloves

SMALL BOUQUET GARNI:

2	sprigs parsley	2
1	bay leaf	1
1	sprig fresh thyme OR oregano, basil, sage, rosemary or ⅛ tsp. (0.5 mL) dried – tied with string into a small cheesecloth bundle	1
6	black peppercorns	6

- Chop vegetables coarsely and put into a stock pot.
- Cover with lightly salted water. Add bouquet garni and peppercorns.
- Bring to a boil; cover; reduce heat to a simmer. Simmer for 2 hours. Strain and cool.
- Stock may be frozen in small containers to be used when needed.

VARIATIONS   Add quartered sweet potatoes and/or white potatoes to the stock. For a slightly sweet stock for pumpkin, squash or corn soups, add a few raisins and a quartered apple or pear.

For a richly flavored **Roasted Vegetable Stock**, use leftover oven-roasted onions, potatoes, parsnips and carrots in the stock.

FISH STOCK

ANY TYPE OF WHITE-FLESHED FISH MAY BE USED TO MAKE THIS STOCK

2 qts.	water	2 L
2 lbs.	white-fleshed, non-oily fish, include heads, bones & skin (cod, pickerel, sole, halibut, bass, flounder, red snapper)	1 kg
½ cup	chopped onion	125 mL
¼ cup	chopped carrot	60 mL
1-2 stalks	celery, chopped	1-2 stalks
1	small bay leaf	1
1-2	garlic cloves, halved	1-2
¼ tsp.	dried thyme flakes	1 mL
3	sprigs parsley	3
6	black peppercorns	6
	salt & pepper to taste	

- Place all ingredients, except salt and pepper, in a stock pot over high heat, cover and bring to a rapid boil. Reduce heat, skim several times then simmer, uncovered, for 20 minutes.
- Strain through a colander lined with 2 thicknesses of cheesecloth. Return any chunks of fish to stock. Add salt and pepper to taste.
- Use stock as directed or refrigerate or freeze, covered, in 1 cup (250 mL) portions for future use. (If freezing, omit chunks of fish.) Can be stored, frozen, up to 3 months.

VARIATIONS   Add 1 cup (250 mL) of white wine.

For a richer stock, cook vegetables in 1 tbsp. (15 mL) of butter, over medium-low heat, until translucent. Do not brown. Add remaining ingredients and cook as above.

Shellfish shells, eg. shrimp, crab or lobster, may be used with fish or instead of fish.

YIELD   *APPROXIMATELY 6 CUPS (1.5 L) STOCK*

CHICKEN STOCK

A LEFTOVER CHICKEN OR TURKEY CARCASS MAY BE USED

3½ lbs.	chicken backs & necks, rinsed	1.75 kg
4 qts.	cold water	4 L
1	large onion, unpeeled, quartered	1
2	carrots, washed	2
2 stalks	celery, leaves included, quartered	2 stalks
4	sprigs parsley	4
4	garlic cloves, halved	4
1 tsp.	salt	5 mL
1 tbsp.	dried thyme	15 mL
10	black peppercorns	10
2	bay leaves	2
½ tsp.	curry powder (optional)	2 mL

- Place chicken and water in a stock pot over medium-high heat.
- Bring to a simmer, skimming foam off the top and discarding.
- Reduce heat to maintain a very gentle simmer. Keep skimming until clear.
- Add remaining ingredients.
- Cover, leaving lid ajar. Simmer for 3 hours.
- Discard bones, any meat and vegetables. Strain stock through a sieve.
- Let cool; refrigerate; remove fat from top of stock.
- Use whenever a recipe calls for chicken stock. Store in the refrigerator for up to 4 days or freeze in smaller containers to be used when needed.

VARIATIONS Omit curry powder and add 1 tbsp. (15 mL) chopped fresh or 1 tsp. (5 mL) dried: basil, sage, rosemary and savory.

YIELD *APPROXIMATELY 3 QUARTS (3 L) STOCK*

BEEF STOCK

YOUR SOUP IS ONLY AS GOOD AS YOUR STOCK!

1 tbsp.	EACH butter & olive oil	15 mL
3-4 lbs.	meaty beef soup bones	1.5-2 kg
2	carrots, chopped	2
1	medium onion, chopped	1
4 cups	water	1 L
1 cup	dry red wine	250 mL
2	bay leaves	2
2 stalks	celery with leaves, chopped	2 stalks
10	black peppercorns	10

- Heat butter and oil in a stock pot; brown meat, carrots and onion.
- Add remaining ingredients; cover. Bring to a boil. Reduce heat and cook at a slow boil until meat is tender, 1½-2 hours.
- Strain through a sieve or cheesecloth-lined colander, reserving meat and stock separately. Cool stock.
- Remove congealed fat from surface of cooled stock.
- Remove meat from bones and chop into bite-sized pieces.
- Freeze any unused stock and meat in separate containers.

VARIATIONS   Add 1 or 2 parsnips, chopped; 1-2 tbsp. (15-30 mL) dried thyme and 6 whole cloves.

For a different flavor, add a 6 oz. (170 mL) can of tomato paste.

YIELD   *APPROXIMATELY 4 CUPS (1 L) STOCK*

COLD CHERRY SOUP

ADD A SPLASH OF KIRSCH IF YOU WISH

2 cups	warm water	500 mL
½ cup	sugar	125 mL
2 tbsp.	lemon juice	30 mL
2 lbs.	fresh cherries, stemmed, pitted, halved	1 kg
1 cup	cherry-flavored yogurt	250 mL

- In a large bowl, dissolve sugar in water. Add lemon juice.
- Reserve a few cherries for garnish. In a food processor, purée remaining cherries with some sugar syrup. Stir purée and yogurt into syrup.
- Chill soup. Serve garnished with cherry halves and additional yogurt.

YIELD   5 – 6 SERVINGS

PEACH SOUP WITH RASPBERRY COULIS

FRESH FRUIT FLAVOR AND SPECTACULAR COLOR

3 lbs.	peaches, peeled, seeded & sliced	1.5 kg
3 cups	peach OR apricot nectar	750 mL
⅓-½ cup	berry (superfine) sugar	75-125 mL
2 cups	fresh raspberries or frozen, thawed	500 mL
¼ cup	berry (superfine) sugar	60 mL
	nutmeg for garnish	
	sour cream OR yogurt for garnish (optional)	
	mint sprigs for garnish	

- In a blender or food processor, purée peaches, peach nectar and sugar; refrigerate.
- Purée raspberries; strain and discard seeds. Stir ¼ cup (60 mL) sugar into raspberry coulis; refrigerate.
- Spoon chilled peach soup into bowls; add 2 large spoonfuls of raspberry coulis and swirl through soup. Sprinkle with nutmeg; garnish with a spoonful of sour cream, if using, and a mint sprig.

YIELD   6 – 7 SERVINGS

ICY PEACH & BLUEBERRY SOUP

BEAUTIFUL PRESENTATION – ALSO DELICIOUS WITH MANGOES OR NECTARINES

1 cup	water	250 mL
¼ tsp.	EACH cinnamon, nutmeg & cloves	1 mL
1-2 tbsp.	sugar	15-30 mL
1 tbsp.	cornstarch	15 mL
¼ cup	water	60 mL
2 lbs.	fresh peaches peeled, pitted OR 28 oz. (796 mL) can sliced peaches	1 kg
1 cup	white wine	250 mL
2 cups	thinly sliced peeled peaches	500 mL
1 cup	sour cream OR plain yogurt for garnish	250 mL
1 cup	blueberries for garnish	250 mL

- In a small saucepan, bring 1 cup (250 mL) water, any juices from sliced or canned peaches, spices and sugar to a boil. Dissolve cornstarch in ¼ cup (60 mL) water; stir into simmering liquid until thickened.
- In a blender or food processor, purée peaches.
- Pour spiced syrup into a large non-metal bowl. Stir in wine, peach purée and sliced peaches. Refrigerate, covered, for several hours.
- Garnish each serving with sour cream and blueberries.

VARIATION   Add ½ cup (125 mL) fresh orange juice and grated zest of 1 orange to peach purée.

YIELD   *6 – 8 SERVINGS*

See photograph on page 17.

BLUEBERRY SOUP

THIS SWEET-TART SWEDISH SOUP IS DELICIOUS FOR BREAKFAST,
LUNCH OR EVEN AS A DESSERT — TRY IT AS A SAUCE ON ICE CREAM

4 cups	fresh blueberries	1 L
2 cups	water	500 mL
2 cups	unsweetened apricot OR pineapple juice	500 mL
3 tbsp.	quick-cooking tapioca	45 mL
2	cloves	2
1	cinnamon stick, halved	1
¼ tsp.	nutmeg	1 mL
½ cup	honey	125 mL
2	lemons, juice of	2
½ cup	lingonberry OR red currant jelly (optional)	125 mL
	plain yogurt OR sour cream for garnish	
	grated orange zest for garnish	
	blueberries & mint sprigs for garnish	

- Rinse blueberries and place in a large saucepan with water, juice, tapioca, cloves, cinnamon and nutmeg. Bring to a boil over medium heat. Stir in honey, reduce heat to low; simmer, covered, until berries are tender, about 15 minutes.
- Remove from heat and stir in lemon juice and jelly. Cover and refrigerate for 4 hours or overnight.
- Serve with a spoonful of yogurt or sour cream, grated orange zest, whole blueberries and mint sprigs.

VARIATIONS   Replace 1 cup (250 mL) of juice with Sauternes or another sweet white wine.

If you prefer, substitute 2 tbsp. (30 mL) of cornstarch for the tapioca.

YIELD   *6 – 8 SERVINGS*

FRESH STRAWBERRY/RASPBERRY SOUP

VIBRANT BERRIES AND ROSÉ OR RED WINE – HEAVENLY!

4 cups	strawberries OR raspberries, or combine them	1 L
½ cup	sugar	125 mL
1 cup	sour cream OR plain yogurt	250 mL
1 cup	whipping cream	250 mL
2½ cups	water	625 mL
1 cup	rosé OR a fruity red wine like Zinfandel OR Beaujolais	250 mL
	sour cream OR yogurt for garnish	
	fresh berries & mint sprigs for garnish	

- In a blender, purée berries with sugar.
- Add sour cream, whipping cream, water and wine and blend well.
- Refrigerate soup, covered, for 4-6 hours.
- Garnish individual servings with a spoonful of sour cream, berries and a mint sprig.

VARIATIONS
- Substitute cran-raspberry juice for the wine.
- Use frozen unsweetened berries if fresh are not available.
- Garnish with fresh blueberries
- If you are counting calories, try low-fat or fat-free sour cream or yogurt and half 'n' half (cereal) cream instead of sour cream and whipping cream.
- Garnish with orange segments, all pith and membranes removed.

YIELD   *4 – 6 SERVINGS*

See photograph on page 17.

STRAWBERRY ORANGE SOUP

SIMPLE, SOPHISTICATED AND SUPERB – A FRESH AND FRUITY SUMMER SOUP

2 qts.	fresh strawberries, washed & hulled	2 L
3 cups	fresh orange juice	750 mL
6 tbsp.	orange-flavored liqueur, Grand Marnier, Cointreau, Triple Sec, etc.	90 mL
3 tbsp.	sugar, or to taste	45 mL
½ cup	EACH sour cream & plain yogurt sliced strawberries & mint sprigs for garnish (optional)	125 mL

- In a blender, purée strawberries until smooth.
- Pour purée into a large bowl; stir in remaining ingredients; blend well.
- Refrigerate soup, covered, for 2-3 hours.
- Garnish each serving with strawberry slices and mint sprigs, if using.

YIELD   6 – 8 SERVINGS

CURRIED PEAR SOUP

CURRY BRINGS OUT THE BEST IN PEARS

3 tbsp.	butter OR margarine	45 mL
1	medium onion, finely chopped	1
½ tsp.	curry powder, or more to taste	2 mL
4	ripe pears, peeled, coarsely chopped	4
3 cups	chicken stock	750 mL
1 tsp.	lemon juice	5 mL

- Melt butter in a large saucepan; add onion and sprinkle with curry powder. Sauté until onion is soft, about 5 minutes.
- Add pears to onion. Add chicken stock and lemon juice; bring to a boil. Cover; reduce heat; simmer for 10 minutes, until pears are very tender.
- In a food processor, purée, half at a time, until very smooth.
- Serve very cold or piping hot.

YIELD   4 – 5 SERVINGS

SCANDINAVIAN FRUIT SOUP

DELICIOUS COLD OR WARM AS A FIRST COURSE OR AS A DESSERT

1 lb.	dried mixed fruit (apples, apricots, peaches, pears)	500 g
1 cup	seedless raisins	250 mL
2	cinnamon sticks	2
6 cups	water	1.5 L
1	orange	1
3 cups	pineapple juice	750 mL
⅔ cup	sugar	150 mL
3 tbsp.	quick-cooking tapioca	45 mL

- In a large, heavy saucepan, combine fruit, raisins, cinnamon and water. Bring to a boil; simmer for 30 minutes.
- Cut orange, with peel, into ½" (1.3 cm) slices. Quarter slices.
- Add orange and remaining ingredients to kettle. Bring to a boil. Cover; reduce heat. Cook for an additional 15 minutes over low heat.
- Refrigerate, covered, for 4-6 hours if serving cold.

YIELD   **6 SERVINGS**

COLD TOMATO & ORANGE SOUP

A REAL SURPRISE – LIGHT, TANGY AND VERY EASY TO MAKE

2 cups	EACH tomato & orange juice	500 mL
½ cup	dry white wine	125 mL
1	lemon, juice of	1
1 tsp.	sugar	5 mL
1½ tsp.	salt	7 mL
¼ tsp.	cayenne pepper	1 mL
	chopped parsley for garnish	

- In a large bowl or pitcher, combine all ingredients, except parsley. Chill.
- Serve very cold, sprinkled with chopped parsley.

YIELD   **6 – 8 SERVINGS**

RED PEPPER SOUP WITH ROASTED TOMATOES

ROASTED TOMATOES ADD RICH FLAVOR TO THIS RED PEPPER SOUP.
SERVE CHILLED OR HOT

3	large red peppers, quartered & seeded	3
2 lbs.	Roma tomatoes, halved lengthwise, seeded & drained	1 kg
1	onion, cut into thin wedges	1
4	garlic cloves	4
2 tbsp.	olive oil	30 mL
	salt and pepper to taste	
1 tbsp.	chopped fresh basil or 1 tsp. (5 mL) dried	15 mL
2 cups	chicken stock	500 mL
1	lemon, juice of (optional), OR 2 tbsp. (30 mL) balsamic vinegar sour cream OR plain yogurt for garnish chopped fresh basil for garnish	1

- Place peppers, tomatoes (cut side up), onion and garlic cloves on a large baking pan. Drizzle oil over; sprinkle liberally with salt and pepper. Roast at 350°F (180°C) until brown and tender, almost charred, about 40-60 minutes; turn peppers and onion occasionally. Remove from oven. Cool.
- Place vegetables and any juices in a food processor. Add basil. Purée soup, gradually adding stock to thin soup to desired consistency. Refrigerate, covered, for 4-6 hours or overnight.
- Top each serving with a spoonful of sour cream. Garnish with chopped basil.

NOTE   Lining the baking pan with foil will ensure easy cleanup.

YIELD   *4 SERVINGS*

Icy Peach & Blueberry Soup, page 11
Sensational Strawberry Salad, page 130
Fresh Strawberry/Raspberry Soup, page 13

CHILLED RED PEPPER SOUP

INTENSE ROASTED PEPPER FLAVOR – AN IDEAL HOT-WEATHER SOUP

4	large red peppers (about 2¼ lbs.)	4
2 tbsp.	olive oil	30 mL
1	onion, coarsely chopped	1
3 cups	chicken stock	750 mL
¼ tsp.	red pepper flakes	1 mL
	salt and pepper to taste	
1 tbsp.	fresh lemon juice	15 mL
	garlic croûtons, see below	
	chopped fresh basil, for garnish	

- Char peppers under a broiler until blackened on all sides. Place in a paper bag and let stand for 10 minutes. Peel and seed; chop coarsely.
- Heat oil in a large saucepan over medium-high heat; add onion and sauté until soft, about 6 minutes. Add peppers and stock. Simmer until vegetables are tender, about 5 minutes.
- Place peppers and onion in a food processor and purée. Add some stock and blend until smooth.
- Stir in pepper flakes, salt, pepper and lemon juice. Refrigerate, covered, for 4-6 hours or overnight.
- Garnish individual servings with croûtons and chopped basil.

VARIATION Substitute bottled roasted red peppers if you wish.

YIELD **4 SERVINGS**

BAKED CROÛTONS

ADDS CRUNCH TO SOUPS AND SALADS

- Brush slices of crusty bread with olive oil. Sprinkle with dried thyme. Cut into ½" (1.3 cm) cubes. Place on a baking sheet and bake at 350°F (180°C), tossing frequently, for 15 minutes, or until crisp.

VARIATIONS For **Oil & Garlic Croûtons**, omit thyme and generously sprinkle cubed bread with garlic powder.
For **Parmesan Garlic Croûtons**, sprinkle Parmesan cheese over Oil & Garlic Croûtons. Bake as above for both variations.

SPICY GAZPACHO

THIS CRUNCHY CHILLED SOUP IS WONDERFULLY REFRESHING

2 lbs.	fresh tomatoes, peeled OR 28 oz. (796 mL) can diced tomatoes	1 kg
1	large green OR red pepper, seeded, finely chopped	1
2-3	garlic cloves, finely chopped	2-3
¾ cup	fresh mixed herbs, chopped (chives, parsley, basil, chervil, tarragon)	175 mL
1	large Spanish onion, finely chopped	1
1	large cucumber, peeled, finely chopped	1
½ cup	vegetable OR olive oil	125 mL
⅓ cup	lemon juice	75 mL
4 cups	tomato juice	1 L
2 tbsp.	red wine vinegar	30 mL
2 tsp.	salt	10 mL
½ tsp.	EACH paprika & black pepper	2 mL
2 tsp.	Worcestershire sauce, or more, to taste	10 mL
1 tsp.	Tabasco sauce, or more, to taste	5 mL
	Oil & Garlic Croûtons, page 19, for garnish	
	chopped fresh herbs for garnish	

- Purée tomatoes in a blender; pour purée into a 4-quart (4 L) glass or plastic container.
- Add chopped pepper, garlic, herbs, onion and cucumber. Stir well. Stir in oil, lemon and tomato juices, vinegar, salt, paprika, pepper, Worcestershire and Tabasco. Cover and chill at least 4 hours, or overnight. Refrigerated, this soup will remain fresh and crunchy for several days.
- Garnish with Oil & Garlic Croûtons and chopped fresh herbs.

VARIATIONS Add ½ lb. (250 g) small cooked shrimp to Gazpacho before serving.
For a summer party try adding 1 oz. (30 mL) vodka to each serving.
Purée or pulse all ingredients for a smooth or slightly textured soup.

YIELD ***10 – 12 SERVINGS***

GREEN GAZPACHO

MANY DELICIOUS VARIETIES OF GAZPACHO ORIGINATED IN SOUTHERN SPAIN

2 cups	coarsely chopped peeled English cucumbers	500 mL
1 cup	chopped romaine lettuce	250 mL
½ cup	coarsely chopped green pepper	125 mL
¼ cup	coarsely chopped onion	60 mL
2 tbsp.	olive oil	30 mL
2 tbsp.	rice OR white wine vinegar	30 mL
¼ tsp.	cumin	1 mL
1 tsp.	salt	5 mL
	cayenne & black pepper to taste	
1-2	garlic cloves, minced	1-2
1 cup	cubed crustless white bread	250 mL
1½ cups	water	375 mL
1	lemon, juice of	1
1	avocado, coarsely chopped	1
½ cup	fresh crab meat (optional)	125 mL
2 tbsp.	minced fresh chives	30 mL
	olive oil for drizzling	

- In a food processor, purée cucumber, lettuce, green pepper, onion, oil, vinegar, seasonings and garlic.
- Add bread and let stand until soggy, about 2 minutes. Purée until smooth.
- Transfer gazpacho to a large bowl and stir in water and lemon juice. Cover and refrigerate for 4-6 hours or overnight.
- Divide gazpacho among 4 bowls. Divide avocado among the bowls. Sprinkle with crab meat and chives; drizzle with oil. Serve immediately.

YIELD   **4 SERVINGS**

WHITE GAZPACHO WITH ALMONDS & GRAPES

AN ELEGANT VERSION OF THE POPULAR SPANISH SOUP

¾ cup	blanched almonds	175 mL
4	garlic cloves, peeled & minced	4
½ tsp.	salt, or more to taste	2 mL
4	slices day-old French bread, crusts removed	4
3 cups	ice water	750 mL
½ cup	olive oil	125 mL
3 tbsp.	white wine vinegar OR lemon juice	45 mL
2 tbsp.	sherry vinegar	30 mL
1½ cups	halved, seedless green grapes, for garnish	375 mL
	Oil & Garlic Croûtons, page 19 (optional)	

- In a food processor or blender, purée almonds, 2 garlic cloves and salt until almonds are very finely ground.
- Soak bread in 1 cup (250 mL) of ice water, then squeeze out water. Add bread to processor. With processor running, slowly add oil and 1 cup (250 mL) of ice water. Add vinegars and process until smooth.
- Place in a glass or plastic bowl; stir in remaining ice water. Adjust seasonings with salt and vinegar. Chill for 4-6 hours.
- Garnish each serving with grapes and croûtons.

VARIATIONS Replace half of the ice water with white grape juice or white wine. Garnish with toasted sliced almonds.

YIELD **4 – 6 SERVINGS**

CHILLED CUCUMBER GARLIC SOUP

THE MIDDLE EASTERN APPETIZER TZATSIKI INSPIRED THIS TANGY, REFRESHING SUMMER SOUP

1	seedless English cucumber, coarsely grated or finely diced	1
3-4 cups	buttermilk OR half buttermilk & half plain yogurt	750 mL-1 L
2 tbsp.	olive oil	30 mL
2 tbsp.	fresh lemon juice	30 mL
2-4	garlic cloves, crushed	2-4
½ tsp.	Tabasco sauce	2 mL
2	green onions, chopped	2
1 tsp.	salt, or more to taste	5 mL
	freshly ground pepper	
2 tbsp.	chopped fresh mint OR dillweed	30 mL
	chopped cucumber & mint OR dill sprigs for garnish (optional)	

- Combine all ingredients, except the garnish, in a large bowl; stir well. Cover and refrigerate overnight.
- Sprinkle individual servings with chopped cucumber and mint or dill.

VARIATION If you prefer a smooth soup, blend all ingredients, except the garnish, in a blender or food processor.

YIELD **4 – 6 SERVINGS**

Celebrated at garlic festivals and in many cookbooks, pungent garlic has been cultivated for over 5,000 years. Regarded as sacred by the pharaohs, it was also used to enhance the strength and endurance of the slaves who built the pyramids and by Greek and Roman soldiers and athletes. Studies have shown that garlic helps to lower LDL cholesterol and boost HDL cholesterol. It is a very good source of Vitamin C and B6, selenium, manganese and anti-inflammatory compounds and has numerous health benefits. Choose plump, firm garlic bulbs with unbroken skin. Store, covered or uncovered, in a cool, dark place.

CHILLED BEET SOUP

QUICK AND REFRESHING WITH A GORGEOUS COLOR

14 oz.	can whole small beets & liquid	398 mL
2	large slices of onion	2
3 cups	beef stock	750 mL
3 tbsp.	Demerara sugar	45 mL
2 tbsp.	fresh lemon juice	30 mL
½ tsp.	salt	2 mL
⅛ tsp.	pepper	0.5 mL
1 cup	sour cream	250 mL
½	large cucumber, peeled & chopped, for garnish	½

- Purée beets with juice and onion in a blender.
- Heat purée with stock in a small saucepan over medium heat. Stir in sugar, lemon juice, salt and pepper. Simmer, uncovered, for 3-4 minutes.
- Allow soup to cool. Stir in sour cream; add salt and pepper to taste. Chill thoroughly, 4-6 hours or overnight.
- Garnish each serving with a spoonful of chopped cucumber.

YIELD   6 – 8 SERVINGS

FRESH ASPARAGUS SOUP

MELLOW, UNBEATABLE FLAVOR

2 tbsp.	vegetable oil	30 mL
1	medium onion, chopped	1
2 stalks	celery, chopped	2 stalks
4 cups	chicken stock	1 L
12 oz.	fresh asparagus spears	340 g
1	large potato, peeled & chopped	1
½ tsp.	salt	2 mL
¼ tsp.	EACH pepper & nutmeg	1 mL
1½ cups	milk	375 mL

FRESH ASPARAGUS SOUP
(CONTINUED)

- In a large saucepan, heat oil; sauté onion and celery until tender. Add chicken stock and bring to a boil.
- Cut tips off asparagus spears; add to stock and cook until tender-crisp, about 2 minutes. Remove tips; run under cold water; set aside.
- Chop remaining asparagus. Add to stock with potato, salt, pepper and nutmeg. Reduce heat; cover and cook until potato is tender.
- Purée soup in a blender or use a hand processor.
- Add milk and reserved tips to purée. Heat until hot but not boiling.

YIELD   ***6 SERVINGS***

CREAM OF LEEK SOUP
THIS VERSION OF THE CLASSIC VICHYSSOISE IS COMFORTING ON A CHILLY DAY

¼ cup	butter	60 mL
1 cup	sliced leeks (white part only)	250 mL
½ cup	chopped onion	125 mL
½ cup	chopped celery	125 mL
4 cups	water	1 L
1 tsp.	salt	5 mL
½ tsp.	pepper	2 mL
2 tbsp.	chopped fresh parsley	30 mL
1	bay leaf	1
2 cups	peeled, diced potatoes	500 mL
1 cup	milk	250 mL

- In a large saucepan, melt butter; sauté leeks, onion and celery. Add water, salt, pepper, parsley and bay leaf. Simmer for 1 hour.
- Add potatoes and cook until tender.
- Add milk. Stir thoroughly. Heat but do NOT boil.
- Remove bay leaf. Serve hot.

VARIATION   Serve very cold; garnish with chopped chives or green onions.

YIELD   ***4 SERVINGS***

LEEK & STILTON SOUP

LUXURIOUS – A RICH AND FLAVORFUL VICHYSSOISE VARIATION

¼ cup	butter	60 mL
2 lbs.	leeks, sliced, white part only	1 kg
1 lb.	potatoes, diced	500 g
1 stalk	celery, thinly sliced	1 stalk
2½ cups	EACH chicken stock & milk	625 mL
	salt & pepper to taste	
1¼ cups	whipping cream	300 mL
⅛ tsp.	nutmeg	0.5 mL
3-4 oz.	Stilton per person, crumbled	75-125 g

- Melt butter in a large saucepan. Add leeks and potatoes. Cook for 7 minutes, stirring continuously. Add celery, stock and milk; bring slowly to a boil. Add seasonings to taste.
- Simmer for 25 minutes, or until vegetables are tender.
- Allow soup to cool. Purée in a blender or food processor.
- Before serving, heat soup gently, do NOT boil. Add Stilton just before serving, or sprinkle soup with Stilton and broil until cheese bubbles.

VARIATIONS   Substitute Gorgonzola, Danish Blue or Roquefort for the Stilton.

YIELD   *4 – 6 SERVINGS*

CREAM OF MUSHROOM SOUP

VERSATILE – SERVE AS A FIRST COURSE OR USE IN YOUR FAVORITE RECIPES

1 lb.	mushrooms	500 g
2 tbsp.	butter	30 mL
4 cups	chicken stock	1 L
1 cup	finely chopped celery	250 mL
½ cup	finely chopped onion	125 mL
¼ cup	chopped parsley	60 mL
1	bay leaf, crushed	1
¼ cup	butter	60 mL
¼ cup	flour	60 mL
2 cups	half 'n' half (cereal) cream	500 mL

CREAM OF MUSHROOM SOUP
(CONTINUED)

- Finely chop half the mushrooms. Slice the other half.
- In a large skillet, sauté mushrooms in butter. Add stock, celery, onion, parsley and bay leaf. Simmer for 20 minutes.
- In a small saucepan, make a white sauce by melting remaining butter. Stir in flour; gradually stir in cream. Cook over low heat, stirring until smooth and thick.
- Add sauce to soup. Cook and stir until thickened.

NOTE   Cool and freeze soup in 1½ cup (375 mL) portions for recipes calling for a can of mushroom soup.
When mushrooms are readily available, double recipe and freeze.

YIELD   ***6 CUPS (1.5 L)***

ZUCCHINI BISQUE
FRESH OR FROZEN, ANOTHER GREAT OPTION FOR ZUCCHINI

2 tbsp.	butter	30 mL
1	medium onion, chopped	1
1 cup	thinly sliced carrots	250 mL
4 cups	diced, unpeeled zucchini	1 L
2 cups	chicken stock	500 mL
2 tbsp.	sugar	30 mL
¼ tsp.	salt	1 mL
4 cups	milk	1 L
	nutmeg OR chopped parsley for garnish	

- Melt butter in a large soup pot. Sauté onion, carrots and zucchini until onion is tender. Stir in stock, sugar and salt. Cover and simmer for 20 minutes, until vegetables are tender.
- In a blender or food processor, purée in batches until smooth.
- Return purée to soup pot; stir in milk and heat through. Garnish.

NOTE   For freezing, pack in serving-size containers. To serve, thaw and add ½ cup (125 mL) whole milk per 1 cup (250 mL) serving.

YIELD   ***8 SERVINGS***

CREAM OF CELERY SOUP

SERVE WITH TOASTED SANDWICHES FOR A COOL-WEATHER SUPPER

1½ cups	chicken stock	375 mL
2 cups	chopped celery	500 mL
½ cup	chopped onion	125 mL
¼ tsp.	EACH dried parsley & tarragon	1 mL
2 tbsp.	butter	30 mL
2 tbsp.	flour	30 mL
¼ tsp.	EACH salt & pepper	1 mL
1 cup	milk	250 mL

- In a large saucepan, combine stock, celery, onion, parsley and tarragon; cook until vegetables are tender.
- In a small saucepan, melt butter. Blend in flour, salt and pepper. Stir in milk gradually. Cook and stir until thickened and bubbly.
- Add sauce to soup. Stir and heat through.

YIELD   3 – 4 SERVINGS

CREAM OF BROCCOLI SOUP

FOR MAXIMUM FLAVOR, SPRINKLE WITH CRUMBLED CHEDDAR OR BLUE CHEESE

2 cups	chopped broccoli, florets & stems	500 mL
1 tbsp.	olive oil	15 mL
2 stalks	celery, chopped	2 stalks
1	medium onion, chopped	1
4 cups	chicken OR vegetable stock	1 L
2 tbsp.	butter	30 mL
2 tbsp.	flour	30 mL
1 cup	half 'n' half (cereal) cream	250 mL
	salt & pepper to taste	
	crumbled Cheddar OR blue cheese for garnish	

Cream of Broccoli Soup

(Continued)

- In a medium saucepan, heat oil over medium heat. Sauté broccoli stem pieces, onion and celery until tender. Add stock and cook for 8-10 minutes. Add broccoli florets.
- In a small saucepan over low heat, melt butter. Add flour and cream. Cook and stir until thickened and bubbly. Stir into soup and heat through. Season to taste. Garnish with cheese.

YIELD   *4 SERVINGS*

Broccoli Buttermilk Soup

TANGY BUTTERMILK SOUP, DELICIOUS HOT OR COLD

2 cups	chopped broccoli, florets & stems	500 mL
2 cups	vegetable OR chicken stock	500 mL
1	medium onion, coarsely chopped	1
1	bay leaf	1
1 tsp.	dried basil	5 mL
½ tsp.	sugar	2 mL
2	garlic cloves, crushed	2
1¾ cups	buttermilk	425 mL
⅛ tsp.	EACH pepper, cayenne & nutmeg	0.5 mL
	salt to taste	
	grated sharp Cheddar OR diced tomato for garnish	

- In a large saucepan, combine broccoli, stock, onion, bay leaf, basil, sugar and garlic. Bring to a boil; reduce heat and cook until broccoli is tender. Discard bay leaf.
- Purée soup in a food processor, a little at a time, until smooth.
- Return purée to the pot and gradually whisk in buttermilk. Heat thoroughly; do NOT boil. Add pepper, cayenne, nutmeg and salt.
- Top each serving with grated Cheddar cheese or diced tomato.

YIELD   *4 – 6 SERVINGS*

CAULIFLOWER SOUP

A LIGHT AND LOVELY SOUP OR APPETIZER

1 tbsp.	butter	15 mL
¼ cup	chopped onion	60 mL
2 cups	finely chopped cauliflower	500 mL
2 cups	chicken stock	500 mL
1 tsp.	dried tarragon	5 mL
1 tsp.	salt	5 mL
½ tsp.	pepper	2 mL
½ cup	milk	125 mL
1 tbsp.	flour	15 mL
	nutmeg for garnish	

- In a large, heavy saucepan, heat butter and sauté onion and cauliflower. Add stock, tarragon, salt and pepper. Let simmer until vegetables are tender.
- Combine milk and flour, stirring until smooth. Add to soup. Simmer until heated through.
- Sprinkle individual servings with nutmeg. Serve hot.

YIELD   3 – 4 SERVINGS

 White, green, purple and now orange – cauliflower is a member of the cabbage family. It is rich in vitamin C and also a fair source of iron. The cauliflower head should be compact and firm. It may be stored in the refrigerator for up to 5 days before cooking. Steamed and puréed with some no-fat half 'n' half or cooked in chicken stock and then puréed, cauliflower makes an excellent substitute for mashed potatoes. Also try it with a bit of curry powder.

CAULIFLOWER STILTON SOUP

MELLOW AND RICH – A COLD WEATHER COMFORT SOUP

¼ cup	butter	60 mL
1	medium onion, chopped	1
2	leeks, white part only, chopped	2
¾ cup	chopped celery	175 mL
4 cups	cauliflower florets	1 L
¼ cup	flour	60 mL
3 cups	chicken OR vegetable stock	750 mL
⅛ tsp.	EACH nutmeg & cayenne	0.5 mL
1 cup	milk OR cream, or more to taste	250 mL
3-4 oz.	Stilton, crumbled	90-115 g
	salt & freshly ground pepper to taste	
	additional Stilton, minced chives or hot	
	pepper sauce for garnish	

- In a heavy large soup pot, over medium heat, melt butter. Add onion, leeks, celery and cauliflower. Cover and cook until onion is translucent, stirring frequently, about 8 minutes. Add flour and stir for 2 minutes.
- Gradually stir in stock, nutmeg and cayenne. Bring to a boil. Reduce heat. Cover and simmer until vegetables are tender and soup thickens, stirring occasionally, about 20 minutes.
- Purée soup in a blender in batches until smooth. Return to soup pot.
- Add milk and heat through, thinning with more milk, if desired. Gradually add Stilton, stirring until melted. Season to taste with salt and pepper.
- Garnish each serving with more Stilton or minced chives and a splash of hot pepper sauce, if desired.

VARIATION Substitute Roquefort, Gorgonzola or Danish Blue for the Stilton or try Gruyère cheese for a milder version.

Add ¼ cup (60 mL) of dry sherry, or more to taste.

Potato Blue Cheese Soup: Substitute 1 lb. (500 g) potatoes for cauliflower.

Add 1-2 cloves garlic, crushed, with the onion.

Garnish this soup with crisp, crumbled bacon.

YIELD *4 – 6 SERVINGS*

CURRIED CAULIFLOWER & APPLE SOUP

SATISFYING AND VERY EASY TO PREPARE

1 tbsp.	butter	15 mL
1	small onion, finely chopped	1
2	garlic cloves, crushed	2
1 tsp.	curry powder, or more to taste	5 mL
1-2	Granny Smith apples, peeled & coarsely chopped	1-2
4 cups	cauliflower florets	1 L
2½ cups	chicken OR vegetable stock	625 mL
¼ cup	whipping cream (optional)	60 mL
	salt & pepper to taste	
	grated old Cheddar cheese, for garnish (optional)	

- In a large saucepan, over medium-low heat, melt butter and cook onion, garlic and curry powder, stirring, until onion is softened.
- Add apple, cauliflower and stock; simmer, covered, until cauliflower is very tender, 20-30 minutes.
- In a blender or food processor, purée soup in batches until very smooth. Return purée to the saucepan. Stir in cream, if using; add salt and pepper. Heat until just hot.

VARIATIONS   Don't purée, if you prefer a chunky soup.

Sprinkle each serving with Oil & Garlic Croûtons, see page 19.

YIELD   ***3 – 4 SERVINGS***

See photograph on page 175.

PARSNIP SOUP WITH APPLE

PARSNIP HAS A NATURAL SWEETNESS THAT IS DELICIOUS IN THIS CREAMY SOUP

¼ cup	butter	60 mL
2	large potatoes, diced	2
4	parsnips, finely chopped	4
4	shallots, finely chopped	4
2	leeks, white part only, sliced	2
1	Granny Smith apple, peeled & coarsely chopped	1
¼ cup	chopped fresh parsley	60 mL
4 cups	chicken OR vegetable stock	1 L
1 cup	apple cider OR dry white wine	250 mL
½ cup	whipping OR half 'n' half cream OR whole milk	125 mL
	salt & pepper to taste	
	minced chives for garnish	

- In a large heavy soup pot, melt butter and sauté potatoes, parsnips, shallots, leeks, apple and parsley over moderate heat, stirring, until leek is softened, about 12 minutes.
- Add stock and simmer, covered, for 20 minutes, or until vegetables are soft.
- In a blender, purée soup in batches.
- Return soup to soup pot and stir in cider, cream, salt and pepper to taste. Heat through, stirring occasionally.
- Serve warm, garnished with minced chives.

VARIATION   Purée only half of the soup if you like a chunkier texture.

YIELD   *6 – 8 SERVINGS*

 The first frost brings out the sweetness in parsnips. Roasting or sautéing caramelizes their natural sugars. They contain fiber, potassium, vitamin C and are a good source of folate. Choose firm, small or medium parsnips. They may be stored in the refrigerator for up to two weeks before cooking.

FRESH TOMATO SOUP

A DELICIOUS AUTUMN TREAT WHEN TOMATOES ARE ABUNDANT!

2 cups	peeled, finely chopped fresh tomatoes	500 mL
1 tsp.	baking soda	5 mL
1 cup	milk	250 mL
¼ tsp.	salt	1 mL
¼ tsp.	pepper	1 mL
1-2 tbsp.	chopped fresh parsley for garnish	15-30 mL

- In a medium saucepan, bring tomatoes to a boil. Reduce heat. Add baking soda; mix well.
- In a small saucepan, heat milk just to boiling point. Add to tomatoes. Simmer slowly until thoroughly heated (do NOT boil soup once milk has been added as it will curdle). Stir in salt and pepper.
- Garnish with parsley. Serve hot.

VARIATION   Add 1-2 tsp. (5-10 mL) sugar to intensify tomato flavor.

YIELD   *2 – 3 SERVINGS; RECIPE IS EASILY DOUBLE OR TRIPLED*

CORN-TOMATO CHOWDER

A GREAT AFTER SKIING OR SKATING TREAT WITH FRESH BISCUITS!

2 tbsp.	butter	30 mL
¼ cup	EACH chopped onion & celery	60 mL
1	garlic clove, minced	1
2 tbsp.	flour	30 mL
2 cups	peeled, chopped, fresh tomatoes	500 mL
2	potatoes, diced	2
1 cup	chicken stock	250 mL
2 cups	milk	500 mL
2 cups	kernel corn	500 mL
½ tsp.	dried thyme	2 mL
	salt & pepper to taste	

CORN-TOMATO CHOWDER

(CONTINUED)

- In a large heavy saucepan, melt butter; sauté onion, celery and garlic. Sprinkle with flour. Stir well.
- Add tomatoes, potatoes and stock. Bring to a boil, reduce heat and simmer until potatoes are tender.
- In a separate saucepan, heat milk; do NOT boil. Stir milk and corn into tomato mixture. Add seasonings. Heat, but do NOT boil. Serve hot.

VARIATIONS Substitute 1 cup (250 mL) diced red pepper for the tomato.
Spicy Corn Chowder, add ½ tsp. (2 mL) EACH cumin and cayenne.
Add a 14 oz. (398 mL) can of rinsed black beans.

YIELD **4 SERVINGS**

CORN-BACON CHOWDER

A GREAT STARTER AFTER A DAY ON THE SLOPES

2 tbsp.	crumbled, crisp bacon (2 slices)	30 mL
1	medium onion, finely chopped	1
2 tbsp.	flour	30 mL
1 cup	milk	250 mL
1 tsp.	salt	5 mL
½ tsp.	Worcestershire sauce	2 mL
2 cups	milk	500 mL
14 oz.	can cream-style OR kernel corn	398 mL

- In 1 tbsp. (15 mL) bacon drippings, in skillet, sauté onion until tender.
- Stir in flour, 1 cup (250 mL) milk, salt and Worcestershire sauce. Cook slowly until thickened. Transfer to a large saucepan.
- To saucepan, add remaining milk, corn and bacon. Bring to a boil, stirring constantly. Cook for 2 minutes. Serve hot.

VARIATIONS Add 3-4 drops hot pepper sauce and/or some finely chopped jalapeño pepper. Garnish each serving with several spoonfuls of grated sharp Cheddar cheese. For a **Corn 'n' Sausage Chowder**, substitute ½ lb. (250 g) pork or spicy Italian sausage for bacon. Fry sausage; cut into ½" (1.3 cm) pieces.

YIELD **4-5 SERVINGS**

Corn Potato Chowder

Thick & rich – an outstanding meal in a bowl

2 tbsp.	vegetable oil	30 mL
1	medium onion, chopped	1
2 stalks	celery, chopped	2 stalks
¼ lb.	sausage, ham OR back bacon, diced	100 g
3 cups	chicken stock	750 mL
3	potatoes, peeled, diced	3
2	cobs of corn OR 12 oz. (341 mL) can of kernel corn	2
¼ tsp.	salt	1 mL
¼ tsp.	pepper	1 mL
½ tsp.	Worcestershire sauce	2 mL
¼ tsp.	hot pepper sauce (optional)	1 mL
1 cup	half 'n' half (cereal) cream	250 mL

- In a large, heavy saucepan, heat oil; sauté onion and celery until tender. Add sausage; sauté a few more minutes.
- Add stock and bring to a boil. Add potatoes.
- Remove corn kernels from the cobs. Add corn, salt, pepper, Worcestershire sauce and hot pepper sauce to soup. Reduce heat; simmer until corn is tender and potatoes no longer hold their shape. Stir well so potatoes break apart and thicken the soup.
- Add cream; heat thoroughly but do NOT boil.

VARIATION   For ***Salmon Chowder***, omit sausage. Corn is optional; use fish stock instead of chicken stock. Add 12 oz. (340 g) salmon fillet OR canned salmon to soup after potatoes have cooked for 10 minutes. Cook fresh salmon for about 10 minutes, or until it flakes readily. Flake salmon and add cream as above. Garnish with dill sprigs.

YIELD   *6 SERVINGS*

POTATO-CHEESE SOUP

SERVE WITH A TOASTED WHOLE-WHEAT BLT SANDWICH

1	large potato, peeled & diced	1
1 cup	water	250 mL
2 cups	beef stock	500 mL
2 cups	milk	500 mL
1 cup	half 'n' half (cereal) cream	250 mL
¼ cup	flour	60 mL
2 tbsp.	butter	30 mL
½ lb.	Cheddar cheese, grated	250 g
1 tbsp.	grated onion	15 mL
¼ tsp.	paprika	1 mL
1 tsp.	salt	5 mL
1 tbsp.	minced parsley	15 mL

- In a 3-quart (3 L) saucepan, cook potato in water. Drain off water; reserve. Put cooked potato through a ricer or sieve.
- Return potato to saucepan, along with reserved potato water, stock, milk and cream. Heat, stirring, for 5 minutes.
- Blend flour and butter together. Add to potato mixture. Stir constantly, while cooking, until mixture thickens and is smooth, about 2-3 minutes.
- Add cheese and onion. Reduce heat. Stir to melt cheese. Add seasonings and parsley. Serve hot.

YIELD   **4 SERVINGS**

One of the most nutrient-dense vegetables, potatoes are an excellent source of complex carbohydrates – a good source of long-term energy. They are high in fiber and are fat and cholesterol free. Potatoes are also rich in potassium, vitamins C and B6.

Broccoli Potato Soup

A HEARTY CHOICE FOR VEGETARIANS

1 tbsp.	olive oil	15 mL
1 cup	chopped broccoli, florets & stems	250 mL
1	medium onion, chopped	1
2 stalks	celery, chopped	2 stalks
3 cups	vegetable stock	750 mL
2	potatoes, peeled & diced	2
½ tsp.	Worcestershire sauce	2 mL
¼ tsp.	hot pepper sauce (optional)	1 mL
½ cup	half 'n' half (cereal) cream	125 mL
	salt & pepper to taste	

- In a large heavy saucepan, heat oil. Sauté broccoli stems, onion and celery until tender. Add stock; cook for 10 minutes.
- Add broccoli florets, potatoes, Worcestershire sauce and pepper sauce. Cook until potatoes no longer hold their shape. Stir well so potatoes break apart and thicken soup.
- Add cream; heat through; do NOT boil. Add salt and pepper.

YIELD   *4 SERVINGS*

Rhubarb Summer Garden Soup

TRY THIS UNUSUAL SOUP WITH FRESH OR FROZEN RHUBARB

5 cups	chopped rhubarb	1.25 L
5 cups	chicken stock	1.25 L
2 tbsp.	EACH chopped fresh parsley & dill	30 mL
1	medium potato, finely chopped	1
1	large carrot, finely chopped	1
1 stalk	celery, finely chopped	1 stalk
1	medium onion, finely chopped	1
1 cup	chopped ham	250 mL
¾ cup	half 'n' half (cereal) cream	175 mL
2 tbsp.	instant blending flour	30 mL
½ tsp.	freshly ground black pepper	2 mL

RHUBARB SUMMER GARDEN SOUP
CONTINUED

- In a large soup pot, cook rhubarb in just enough water to cover. Bring to a boil. Drain water off rhubarb, then add chicken stock.
- Add remaining ingredients, except cream, flour and pepper. Simmer for approximately 1 hour, or until vegetables are tender.
- Add cream, flour and pepper. Bring just to the boiling point. Serve hot.

YIELD   *6 – 8 SERVINGS*

PEANUT SOUP WITH SWEET POTATOES

CHUNKY OR PURÉED, THIS AFRICAN GROUND NUT SOUP IS HEARTY & FLAVORFUL

2 tbsp.	vegetable oil	30 mL
2	large onions, diced	2
2	large red peppers, diced	2
2 tsp.	minced fresh ginger	10 mL
3	large garlic cloves	3
2	sweet potatoes, peeled & cubed	2
	salt & freshly ground black pepper	
1 tsp.	EACH red pepper flakes & cumin	5 mL
2 cups	crushed tomatoes	500 mL
5 cups	chicken OR vegetable stock	1.25 L
½-¾ cup	peanut butter	125-175 mL
1 cup	whipping OR half 'n' half (cereal) cream	250 mL
2 cups	cooked rice	500 mL
1 cup	sliced green onion	250 mL

- In a large soup pot, over high heat, heat oil; add onions, peppers, ginger, garlic and sweet potatoes. Sauté and stir until onions begin to brown, 8-10 minutes. Add salt, pepper, pepper flakes and cumin.
- Stir in tomatoes and stock, bring to a boil; lower heat and simmer, covered, for 25 minutes. Stir in peanut butter until it dissolves.
- In a blender, purée 2 cups (500 mL) soup until smooth, or purée all of the soup. Return purée to soup pot; stir in cream; check for seasoning.
- Place 3-4 spoonfuls rice in each bowl. Add soup; sprinkle with onion.

YIELD   *6 SERVINGS*

Avgolemono

A classic Greek egg & lemon soup – tart & terrific

8 cups	chicken stock	2 L
1 cup	orzo OR long-grain rice	250 mL
4	eggs, separated	4
3	lemons, juice of, adjust to taste	3
	salt & freshly ground pepper to taste	
	minced parsley for garnish	
	lemon slices for garnish	

- In a large saucepan, bring stock to a boil. Add orzo or rice and cook until tender, about 15 minutes.
- In a medium bowl, beat egg whites until soft peaks form. Beat in yolks and lemon juice until thoroughly blended.
- Beat in 2 cups (500 mL) stock; pour in slowly and beat continuously to temper eggs. Whisk eggs into soup. Add salt and pepper.
- Serve hot; garnish with parsley and lemon slices.
- To reheat soup, do NOT boil; heat slowly or soup may curdle.

VARIATIONS   Add 1-2 cups (250-500 mL) shredded cooked chicken or turkey. For a much less authentic, but delicious, variation stir in 3-4 cups (750 mL-1 L) shredded fresh spinach leaves just before whisking in the eggs.
Serve soup chilled, with parsley and lemon garnish.

YIELD   *6 – 8 SERVINGS*

French Onion Soup

An international classic – the secret is caramelizing the onions and using good beef stock

1	large onion, sliced	1
2 tbsp.	butter	30 mL
3 cups	beef stock	750 mL
¼ tsp.	salt	1 mL
⅛ tsp.	pepper	0.5 mL
2	slices French bread, toasted	2
½ cup	shredded Swiss or Gruyère cheese	125 mL

French Onion Soup
(Continued)

- In a skillet, sauté onion slices in butter, over medium heat, until tender and translucent. Cook and stir to prevent burning; onions should start to brown after 15 minutes. Reduce heat, and cook, covered, stirring frequently, until onions are caramelized, 30-40 minutes.
- Add stock, salt and pepper. Bring to a boil. Reduce heat and simmer for 15 minutes.
- Pour hot soup into individual ovenproof bowls. Top with toast. Sprinkle with cheese. Broil for 2-3 minutes, until cheese is melted.

VARIATIONS For a vegetarian version, use a roasted vegetable stock.
Add a spoonful of sherry to each bowl before topping with toasted bread.

YIELD **2 SERVINGS**

See photograph on page 139

Onion & Garlic Soup with Beer
Zesty garlic & robust beer flavors make this onion soup special

2 tbsp.	vegetable oil	30 mL
8-10	onions, thinly sliced	8-10
4	large garlic cloves, crushed	4
12 oz.	lager beer OR dark ale	341 mL
5 cups	beef stock (not consommé)	1.25 L
1 tbsp.	sugar, or more to taste	15 mL
	salt & pepper to taste	
	grated Parmesan OR Gruyère cheese for garnish	
	Croûtons, see page 19, for garnish	

- In a large, heavy soup pot, heat oil; cook onions and garlic over moderate heat, stirring occasionally, until browned. Stir in beer and stock.
- Simmer, covered, for 45 minutes. Stir in sugar, salt and pepper to taste.
- Top individual servings with grated cheese and croûtons.

VARIATION Use a sourdough or rye bread for the croûtons.

YIELD **6 – 8 SERVINGS**

GARLIC & WHITE WINE SOUP

DON'T WAIT UNTIL YOU HAVE A COLD TO TRY THIS FLAVORFUL CURE-CALL

¼ cup	butter	60 mL
½ cup	chopped garlic	125 mL
1½ cups	thinly sliced onions	375 mL
½ cup	flour	125 mL
6 cups	beef stock	1.5 L
1 cup	dry white wine	250 mL
½ tsp.	salt	2 mL
½ cup	sour cream OR plain yogurt	125 mL
	nutmeg	
	salt & pepper	
	Garlic Croûtons, page 19, for garnish	
	minced fresh parsley for garnish	

- In a large soup pot, melt butter; sauté garlic and onions over medium heat until golden. Add flour and cook, stirring, for 3 minutes.
- Add stock, wine and salt. Bring to a boil and simmer for 20 minutes.
- Strain soup. (Soup can be made ahead to this point and refrigerated.)
- Reheat soup; stir in sour cream, nutmeg, salt and pepper to taste.
- Garnish individual servings with croûtons and parsley.

YIELD   *6 – 7 SERVINGS*

SPICY GARLIC SOUP

SOPA DA AJO IN SPAIN, SOPA ALENTEJANA IN PORTUGAL, AIGO BOUIDO IN PROVENCE, GARLIC SOUP IS A MEDITERRANEAN FAVORITE

3 tbsp.	olive oil	45 mL
6	garlic cloves, finely chopped	6
4-6 slices	French or Italian bread, ¼" (6 mm) thick	4-6 slices
1 tbsp.	paprika	15 mL
¼ tsp.	EACH ground cumin & cayenne pepper	1 mL
6 cups	chicken OR beef stock	1.5 mL
	salt & pepper to taste	
4-6	eggs – 1 for each serving (optional)	4-6
	chopped fresh parsley for garnish	

Spicy Garlic Soup

(Continued)

- Heat oil in a large heavy soup pot. Add garlic; sauté, stirring, over medium heat until golden. Do not brown. Remove and set aside.
- Add the bread slices, 1 at a time, to the hot oil. Brown on both sides; remove and keep warm.
- Stir paprika into remaining oil in soup pot. Add cumin and cayenne. Stir in stock, garlic and salt. Simmer soup for about 10 minutes.
- Ladle soup into 4-6 ovenproof bowls placed on a baking pan. Bake at 400°F (200°C) until soup simmers.
- Crack eggs and slide 1 egg into each bowl. Top with toasted bread and bake for about 4 minutes, until eggs are set. Yolks should be soft.
- Garnish each serving with parsley.

YIELD   *4 – 6 SERVINGS*

Garlic Soup with Tomatoes & Peppers

GARLIC SOUP IS A TRADITIONAL CURE FOR COLDS. FRESH TOMATOES & PEPPERS ADD MORE NUTRITION AND GORGEOUS COLOR.

½ cup	olive oil	125 mL
3	medium tomatoes, coarsely chopped	3
12	garlic cloves, coarsely chopped	12
2	red peppers, coarsely chopped	2
2 tsp.	salt, OR to taste	10 mL
2 cups	chicken OR vegetable stock	500 mL
	freshly ground black pepper, to taste	
4 slices	French OR Italian bread, lightly toasted	4 slices
	chopped basil OR pesto for garnish	

- In a medium saucepan, heat oil over medium heat; add tomatoes, garlic and peppers; cook, stirring occasionally, for 5 minutes. Stir in salt, stock and pepper. Bring to a boil. Lower heat; simmer for 10 minutes.
- To serve, place a slice of toast in each soup bowl. Pour soup over; add garnish and let sit for 10 minutes before serving.

VARIATIONS   Add ¼ tsp. (1 mL) EACH dried sage, rosemary and thyme as the soup simmers. Garnish each serving with grated Gruyère cheese.

YIELD   *4 SERVINGS*

Tomato, Spinach & Garlic Soup

FULL OF FLAVOR – AN INSTANT FAVORITE! SERVE HOT OR CHILLED

1 tbsp.	olive oil	15 mL
4	garlic cloves, minced	4
½ cup	finely chopped onion	125 mL
3 cups	vegetable stock	750 mL
28 oz.	can EACH crushed & diced tomatoes	796 mL
	salt & pepper to taste	
3 cups	coarsely chopped fresh spinach	750 mL

- In a large soup pot, heat oil and add garlic and onion. Sauté over medium-low heat until onion is translucent.
- Stir in stock and tomatoes; simmer for 15 minutes. Add salt and pepper.
- Stir in spinach; simmer until spinach is wilted, 4-5 minutes.

VARIATIONS   Add ¼ cup (60 mL) chopped fresh basil with the spinach. For a hearty soup, add 28 oz. (796 mL) can of lentils, mixed beans or chickpeas. Garnish with Baked Croûtons, page 19, if you wish.

YIELD   **6 – 8 SERVINGS**

Tuscan Tomato & Bread Soup

A GREAT, COLORFUL PEASANT-STYLE SOUP

⅓ cup	olive oil	75 mL
1 cup	finely chopped onion	250 mL
4	garlic cloves, crushed	4
½ tsp.	red pepper flakes (optional)	2 mL
6 lbs.	ripe tomatoes, peeled, chopped OR	3 kg
	3 x 28 oz. (796 mL) cans plum tomatoes	
28 oz.	can cannellini (white kidney beans) optional	796 mL
½ cup	chopped fresh basil	125 mL
1 qt.	chicken OR vegetable stock	1 L
	salt & pepper to taste	
1	Italian loaf, cut into ¼" (6 mm) slices	1
2 tbsp.	Parmesan cheese	30 mL
	olive oil & Parmesan cheese for garnish	

TUSCAN TOMATO & BREAD SOUP
(CONTINUED)

- In a large heavy soup pot, heat oil and sauté onion until translucent. Stir in garlic and red pepper flakes, if using. Cook for 2-3 minutes.
- Stir in tomatoes and beans, basil, stock, salt and pepper. Simmer, covered, for 10-15 minutes.
- Crumble bread into bite-sized pieces and stir into soup.
- Remove soup from heat; cover and set aside for about 1 hour. Stir in Parmesan just before serving. Serve at room temperature or warm.
- Drizzle with olive oil and sprinkle with Parmesan cheese.

VARIATION Roasting tomatoes first adds a smoky sweet flavor. For **Roasted Tomato Soup**, brush halved Roma tomatoes with olive oil, place skin side up in a shallow pan. Broil until skin is charred, turn tomatoes and broil until browned and bubbly. Proceed as above. Garnish with chopped fresh basil.

YIELD *6 – 8 SERVINGS*

SWEET POTATO MANGO SOUP
AN INTERESTING COMBINATION THAT STIRS THE SENSES

1 tbsp.	vegetable oil	15 mL
1	medium onion, chopped	1
½ tsp.	EACH curry powder & ground cumin	2 mL
3 cups	vegetable stock	750 mL
12 oz.	sweet potato, diced	340 g
1	carrot, coarsely grated	1
1 stalk	celery, chopped	1 stalk
¼ tsp.	salt	1 mL
1	very ripe mango, peeled	1
	yogurt for garnish	

- In a heavy-bottomed saucepan, heat oil over medium heat. Add onion, curry and cumin; stir. Cook until onion is translucent.
- Add stock, potato, carrot, celery and salt. Bring to a boil. Reduce heat to medium; cook until vegetables are tender.
- Remove soup from heat. Purée in a food processor. Add mango and purée.
- Reheat soup and serve hot, topped with a dollop of yogurt.

YIELD *4 SERVINGS*

ROASTED PARSNIP & PEAR SOUP

THE CARAMELIZED FLAVORS OF THE ROASTED VEGETABLES AND PEAR ADD
RICHNESS AND DEPTH TO THIS LOVELY SOUP

1 lb.	parsnips, cut into eighths	500 g
1	yellow pepper, cubed	1
2	garlic cloves, chopped	2
1	potato, cut into 8 wedges	1
1	onion, cut into 8 wedges	1
1-2	pears, peeled, cored, quartered	1-2
2 tbsp.	vegetable oil	30 mL
2-3 cups	vegetable stock, or more	500-750 mL
	salt & pepper to taste	
	cayenne OR hot pepper sauce to taste	

- Place vegetables and pear in a roasting pan; drizzle and rub with oil. Roast at 400°F (200°C) for 20-30 minutes, until browned and tender. Turn once or twice as they roast. If some pieces are getting too brown, remove them from the pan.
- In a food processor, purée the vegetables and pear.
- Place the purée in a large saucepan and stir in vegetable stock until desired consistency is reached. Stir in seasonings to taste.

YIELD   4–5 SERVINGS

Sweet and succulent, pears are high in soluble fiber (pectin) and low in carbs. They have a low glycemic index. They are also a good source of vitamin C and potassium. In soups or roasted with parsnips or other vegetables, pears are very versatile, adding luscious flavor to many savory dishes.

CURRIED SQUASH SOUP WITH PEARS

PEARS ADD A TOUCH OF SWEETNESS TO THIS SMOOTH, FLAVORFUL CURRIED SOUP

1 tbsp.	vegetable oil	15 mL
2 cups	diced onion	500 mL
2	garlic cloves, minced	2
1 tbsp.	curry powder, or more to taste	15 mL
1 tbsp.	brown sugar	15 mL
½ tsp.	cumin, or more to taste	2 mL
½ tsp.	EACH cinnamon & nutmeg	2 mL
6 cups	chicken OR vegetable stock	1.5 L
8 cups	butternut squash, peeled & diced	2 L
2	ripe pears, peeled, cored & diced	
	salt & pepper to taste	
	chopped fresh cilantro OR parsley for garnish	
	sour cream OR yogurt for garnish (optional)	

- In a large soup pot, over medium heat, heat oil. Add onion and cook until soft, about 5 minutes. Add garlic, curry powder, sugar, cumin, cinnamon and nutmeg; stir for about a minute; stir in stock, squash and pears. Bring to a boil; reduce heat and simmer, covered, until squash and pears are tender, about 25 minutes.
- In a food processor or blender, purée the soup in batches.
- Return soup to the soup pot to heat through. Add salt and pepper to taste.
- Serve warm, garnished with cilantro. Add a dollop of sour cream to each serving, if you wish.

VARIATIONS   Add ¼-½ tsp. (1-2 mL) ground ginger with the spices.

                      Add ⅛ tsp. (0.5 mL) cayenne pepper, or more to taste.

YIELD   ***6 – 8 SERVINGS***

CARROT & RUTABAGA SOUP

EARTHY SPICES MAKE THIS A SATISFYING COMFORT SOUP

2 tbsp.	butter	30 mL
1	medium onion, chopped	1
2	carrots, coarsely grated	2
1 lb.	rutabaga, peeled & diced	500 g
4 cups	vegetable stock	1 L
½ tsp.	salt	2 mL
¼ tsp.	pepper	1 mL
¼ tsp.	ground nutmeg	1 mL
2 tsp.	ground coriander	10 mL
1 tsp.	ground cumin	5 mL
2 tsp.	dried crushed cilantro	10 mL
	garlic bread OR croûtons	

- In a heavy bottomed saucepan, melt butter over medium heat. Add onion, carrot and rutabaga. Cook gently for 5 minutes, stirring occasionally.
- Add vegetable stock, salt and pepper. Bring to a boil. Simmer, covered, for 30 minutes, or until vegetables are tender.
- Remove from heat. Purée; return to saucepan. Add nutmeg, coriander, cumin and cilantro. Reheat gently.
- Serve hot with garlic bread or sprinkle with croûtons.

YIELD   *4 SERVINGS*

 Rutabagas vs. turnips: Rutabagas are often called yellow-skinned turnips or Swedes. Related to the cabbage, they contain vitamins A and C. Also a cruciferous vegetable, turnips have white skin with a pale purple top. The flavor is slightly sweet when they are young. Choose both rutabagas and turnips that are heavy for their size.

BORSCH (BEET SOUP)

A UKRAINIAN, GERMAN, POLISH AND RUSSIAN TRADITION
EVERYBODY'S FAVORITE!

4 cups	diced beets	1 L
1 cup	diced carrots	250 mL
4 cups	beef stock	1 L
4 cups	water	1 L
1	large onion, chopped	1
1	garlic clove, minced	1
1 tbsp.	lemon juice OR vinegar	15 mL
2 cups	diced potatoes	500 mL
2 cups	shredded cabbage	500 mL
2 tbsp.	finely chopped fresh dillweed	30 mL
1 tsp.	salt	5 mL
½ tsp.	pepper	2 mL
1 cup	whipping cream	250 mL

- Place beets and carrots in a large kettle with stock and water. Bring to a boil. Add onion, garlic and lemon juice. Simmer until beets and carrots are tender, about 30 minutes.
- Add potatoes. Continue to simmer until potatoes are tender, about 15 minutes.
- Add cabbage, dillweed, salt and pepper. Continue to simmer until cabbage is tender, about 15 minutes. Extra water may be added at this point to obtain desired consistency.
- Add cream just prior to serving. Stir to heat. Do NOT boil soup once cream has been added or it will curdle.

NOTE   The above ingredients serve only as a guide. They may be added to, omitted or decreased as desired. Many people add a spoonful of sour cream to each serving of Borsch.

VARIATIONS   The cook with limited time may wish to substitute 2 cans of cooked, diced beets for the raw beets and adjust the cooking method accordingly.

YIELD   **8 SERVINGS**

MOROCCAN LENTIL CHICKPEA SOUP

CINNAMON, GINGER AND SAFFRON ADD RICH AROMAS AND FLAVOR

2 tbsp.	vegetable oil	30 mL
1	large onion, diced	1
3 stalks	celery, diced	3 stalks
½ cup	chopped fresh parsley	125 mL
1½ tsp.	turmeric	7 mL
1 tsp.	ground cinnamon	5 mL
¼ tsp.	ground ginger	1 mL
14 oz.	can lentils, rinsed & drained OR 1 cup (250 mL) dried lentils	398 mL
14 oz.	can chickpeas, rinsed & drained	398 mL
28 oz.	can diced tomatoes	796 mL
6 cups	chicken OR vegetable stock	1.5 L
pinch	saffron threads	pinch
1 tsp.	pepper	5 mL
	salt to taste	

- In a large heavy soup pot, heat oil; add onion; sauté until onion is translucent. Stir in celery, parsley and turmeric; cook for 2-3 minutes. Stir in remaining ingredients.
- Simmer, covered, over low heat for 25-30 minutes (up to 45 minutes if using dried lentils).

VARIATIONS   Add 2 tbsp. (30 mL) fresh lemon juice, or more to taste.

Add 4 oz. (115 g) angel hair pasta to soup about 5 minutes before serving. Cook until pasta is just al dente.

YIELD   ***6 – 8 SERVINGS***

Spicy Chickpea, Pasta & Sausage Soup, page 60
Tomato Tortellini Soup, page 57
Tomato Mozzarella Salad, page 147

CURRIED LENTIL SOUP

HEARTY AND SATISFYING, A TRUE COLD-WEATHER COMFORT DISH

2 tbsp.	vegetable oil	30 mL
1	large onion, diced	1
2 stalks	celery, sliced	2 stalks
1	carrot, diced	1
3	garlic cloves, crushed	3
1 tbsp.	curry powder, or more to taste	15 mL
½ tsp.	ground cumin	2 mL
28 oz.	can diced tomatoes	796 mL
4-6 cups	chicken OR vegetable stock	1-1.5 L
2 cups	dried red OR green lentils OR 19 oz. (540 mL) canned lentils, rinsed & drained	500 mL
2 tsp.	salt, or more to taste	10 mL
¼ tsp.	freshly ground pepper	1 mL

- In a large soup pot, heat oil; add onion, celery, carrot and garlic. Cook over medium heat until onion is translucent.
- Stir in curry powder and cumin; cook until aromatic, about 1 minute. Stir in tomatoes, stock and lentils. Cook until lentils are tender, about 30-45 minutes (about 20 minutes if using canned lentils).
- Add more stock, if needed; add salt and pepper.
- Serve hot.

VARIATION If you prefer, omit curry powder and double the amount of cumin. Stir in 2 tbsp. (30 mL) lemon juice just before serving.

YIELD **6 SERVINGS**

 Lentils are rich in complex carbohydrates and have a low glycemic index. They contain both soluble fiber and insoluble fiber. They are excellent sources of potassium and folic acid and good sources of other B vitamins and vegetable protein. Lentils cook rapidly, 15-40 minutes depending on the variety, and do not require presoaking.

CURRIED PEANUT SOUP

CURRY ADDS A "BITE" TO CREAMY PEANUT BUTTER

1 tbsp.	vegetable oil	15 mL
1	medium onion, diced	1
1 stalk	celery, sliced	1 stalk
3	garlic cloves, crushed	3
3 tbsp.	curry powder	45 mL
½ tsp.	red pepper flakes, or more to taste	2 mL
4-5 cups	chicken stock	1-1.25 L
⅓ cup	rice	75 mL
3	medium carrots, sliced	3
½ cup	creamy peanut butter	125 mL
1-2 tsp.	sugar	5-10 mL
	salt & pepper to taste	
	finely chopped green onions for garnish	
	chopped fresh parsley for garnish	

- In a large saucepan, over medium-high heat, heat oil. Add onion, celery garlic, curry powder and red pepper flakes. Sauté until onion is translucent, about 5 minutes. Add stock and bring to a boil. Stir in rice and carrots. Reduce heat; simmer until rice is tender, stirring occasionally, about 20 minutes.
- Purée half or all of the soup in a food processor with the peanut butter. Return soup to saucepan and heat through. Do NOT boil. Thin with more stock to desired consistency. Stir in sugar and salt and pepper to taste.
- Garnish individual servings with green onions and parsley.

VARIATIONS   Add 1 cup (250 mL) diced, peeled tomatoes.

For **Creamy Curried Peanut Soup**, substitute 1 cup (250 mL) of coconut milk or whipping cream for 1 cup (250 mL) of stock.

Garnish with chopped dry or honey-roasted salted peanuts.

YIELD   *4 SERVINGS*

MINESTRONE

SERVE WITH A CRUSTY ROLL AND A PIECE OF CHEESE, AND DINNER IS COMPLETE

2 tbsp.	butter	30 mL
1	medium onion, chopped	1
2 stalks	celery, chopped	2 stalks
4 cups	chicken stock	1 L
2	carrots, finely chopped	2
1	bay leaf	1
½ tsp.	ground oregano	2 mL
½ tsp.	garlic powder	2 mL
½ tsp.	salt	2 mL
½ tsp.	pepper	2 mL
28 oz.	can tomatoes	796 mL
⅔ cup	uncooked shell pasta	150 mL
	Parmesan cheese for garnish	

- In a skillet, heat butter and sauté onion and celery until soft. Transfer to a large soup pot.
- Add remaining ingredients, except Parmesan cheese. Heat to boiling. Reduce heat. Simmer until vegetables and pasta are well cooked, about 20-30 minutes.
- Remove bay leaf. Serve hot. Sprinkle with Parmesan cheese.

YIELD   **6 SERVINGS**

The French called them "love apples", but these South American natives only gained true popularity in the 1900s. Tomatoes are rich in antioxident vitamins C, E, beta-carotene and lycopene. Studies indicate that lycopene may help reduce heart disease and some cancers, especially prostate cancer. Cooked or canned tomatoes contain even more lycopene than raw. They are also good sources of vitamin B, potassium, iron, phosphorus and fiber.

PIZZA SOUP
A GUARANTEED HIT

1 tbsp.	vegetable oil	15 mL
2	garlic cloves, minced	2
1	medium onion, chopped	1
½	green pepper, chopped	½
1 cup	sliced fresh mushrooms	250 mL
28 oz.	can tomatoes	796 mL
8 oz.	pepperoni, thinly sliced	250 g
3 cups	beef stock	750 mL
½ tsp.	dried basil	2 mL
⅔ cup	dry elbow macaroni OR small pasta	150 mL
	salt & pepper to taste	
	shredded mozzarella cheese	

- In a large saucepan, heat oil and sauté garlic, onions, pepper and mushrooms until vegetables are tender, about 5 minutes.
- Add tomatoes, pepperoni, stock, basil and macaroni. Bring to a boil; reduce heat; simmer until macaroni is tender. Add salt and pepper.
- Serve hot, sprinkled with mozzarella.

YIELD   *6 SERVINGS*

TORTELLINI SPINACH SOUP
GARLIC AND HERBS ENHANCE THE FRESH FLAVOR OF SPINACH

1 tbsp.	olive oil	15 mL
2	carrots, grated	2
1	medium onion, chopped	1
2	garlic cloves, minced	2
8 cups	chicken stock	2 L
12 oz.	pkg. fresh tortellini	340 g
6 oz.	pkg. fresh baby spinach	170 g
1 tsp.	EACH crushed sweet basil & oregano	2 mL
	salt & pepper to taste	
	shredded mozzarella cheese (optional)	

TORTELLINI SPINACH SOUP
(CONTINUED)

- In a Dutch oven, heat oil. Sauté carrots, onion and garlic until tender. Add the stock; bring to a boil.
- Add tortellini; boil gently for 4 to 5 minutes. Add spinach and seasonings; simmer 2 to 3 minutes, or until spinach is tender.
- Serve hot, sprinkled with mozzarella, if desired.

YIELD   **6 SERVINGS**

TOMATO TORTELLINI SOUP
HEARTY AND OH SO SATISFYING!

2 tbsp.	olive oil	30 mL
1	medium onion, chopped	1
2 stalks	celery, chopped	2 stalks
1	green OR red pepper, chopped	1
2	garlic cloves, minced	2
3 cups	vegetable stock	750 mL
28 oz.	can Italian-style tomatoes	796 mL
12 oz.	fresh beef tortellini pasta	340 g
1 tsp.	dried crushed basil	5 mL
½ tsp.	dried crushed oregano	2 mL
	salt & pepper to taste	
	vegetable stock OR tomato juice	
	freshly grated Parmesan cheese	

- In a large saucepan, heat oil. Sauté onion, celery, pepper and garlic. Add stock and tomatoes; simmer gently to break up tomatoes.
- Add pasta and seasonings. Cook until pasta is still slightly firm.
- Add additional stock or juice to obtain desired consistency.
- To serve, adjust seasonings; sprinkle each serving with Parmesan cheese.

VARIATION   Add 6 oz. (170 g) fresh baby spinach for the last 2-3 minutes of cooking.

YIELD   **6 – 8 SERVINGS**

See photograph on page 51.

Italian Wedding Soup

A DELICIOUS QUICK LUNCHEON DISH IF MEATBALLS ARE
MADE IN ADVANCE AND FROZEN

MEATBALLS:

1 lb.	lean ground beef	500 g
1	egg, slightly beaten	1
½ cup	bread crumbs	125 mL
2 tsp.	Worcestershire sauce	10 mL
1 tsp.	garlic powder	5 mL
2 tsp.	grated Parmesan cheese	10 mL
½ tsp.	dried crushed oregano	2 mL
½ tsp.	dried crushed basil	2 mL
½ tsp.	salt	2 mL
¼ tsp.	pepper	1 mL
1 tbsp.	olive oil	15 mL
4 cups	chicken stock	1 L
6 oz.	fresh spinach, chopped	175 g
½ cup	acini di pepe* OR other confetti-like small pasta	125 g
	Parmesan cheese for garnish	

- Combine meatball ingredients. Shape into ⅓" (1 cm) balls.
- In a large heavy saucepan, heat oil. Add meatballs and brown.
- Add stock, spinach and pasta. Bring to a boil, reduce heat and simmer for 8-10 minutes.
- Serve hot, sprinkled with Parmesan cheese.

NOTE * Acini di pepe (peppercorns) are a very small rice-shaped pasta.

YIELD *6 SERVINGS*

ITALIAN PASTA & WHITE BEAN SOUP
(PASTA E FAGIOLI)

A VERSATILE HEARTY WINTER SOUP THAT IS A MEAL IN ITSELF!

1 cup	dried cannellini OR white kidney beans	250 mL
	water	
1 tbsp.	vegetable oil	15 mL
1 lb.	ground beef	500 g
1	onion, chopped	1
1	carrot, chopped	1
2 stalks	celery, chopped	2 stalks
4	plum tomatoes, peeled, seeded, chopped	4
4 cups	beef stock	1 L
2 tsp.	dried oregano	10 mL
1 tsp.	EACH pepper & salt	5 mL
1 tbsp.	chopped fresh parsley	15 mL
½-1 tsp.	hot pepper sauce	2-5 mL
½ cup	small dry pasta	125 mL
	additional beef stock OR tomato juice	
	freshly grated Parmesan cheese	

- Soak beans overnight in water to cover; drain. In a stockpot, cook beans in water to cover until almost tender, about 1 hour. Drain; return beans to pot.
- In a skillet, heat oil; sauté beef until browned. Add onion, carrot, celery and tomatoes; simmer for 10 minutes, or until vegetables are soft.
- To beans in stockpot, add beef and sautéed vegetables, beef stock and seasonings. Cook over low heat for 30 minutes.
- Add pasta and cook for about 10 minutes, or until pasta is still slightly firm. Add additional stock or juice if soup is too thick.
- To serve, adjust seasonings; sprinkle each serving with Parmesan cheese.

YIELD   *8 – 10 SERVINGS*

BEEF PASTA TOMATO SOUP

SERVE TO HUNGRY FRIENDS WITH A VARIETY OF WHOLE-GRAIN BREADS

1 tbsp.	olive oil	15 mL
1 lb.	ground lean beef	500 g
1	medium onion, chopped	1
½	green pepper, chopped	½
2 stalks	celery, chopped	2 stalks
6 cups	beef stock	1.5 L
28 oz.	can tomatoes	796 mL
	salt & pepper to taste	
1 tsp.	EACH dried crushed oregano & basil	5 mL
1 cup	dry macaroni OR small pasta shapes	250 mL
	beef stock OR tomato juice (optional)	

- In a large heavy saucepan, heat oil and brown beef. Add onion, pepper and celery; cook until onions are translucent.
- Add remaining ingredients; simmer until pasta is tender. Add additional liquid if needed.

YIELD   *8 – 10 SERVINGS*

SPICY CHICKPEA, PASTA & SAUSAGE SOUP

A REAL MEAL IN A BOWL — ZESTY AND FLAVORFUL

2 tbsp.	vegetable oil	30 mL
1 lb.	hot Italian sausages OR chorizo	500 g
1½ tsp.	dried rosemary	7 mL
1 tsp.	dried oregano OR basil	5 mL
2-3	large garlic cloves, crushed	2-3
½ tsp.	dried red pepper flakes	2 mL
28 oz.	can diced tomatoes	796 mL
28 oz.	can chickpeas	796 mL
6 cups	chicken stock	1.5 L
2 cups	small pasta (bows, shells, orzo, etc.)	500 mL
	salt & pepper to taste	
1 cup	grated Parmesan cheese, for garnish	250 mL

SPICY CHICKPEA, PASTA & SAUSAGE SOUP
(CONTINUED)

- In a large soup pot, heat oil over medium heat. Add sausage, rosemary, oregano, garlic and pepper flakes. Sauté until sausages are cooked, 8-10 minutes. Cut sausages into ¼" (6 mm) slices. Return to soup pot.
- Stir in tomatoes, chickpeas, stock and pasta. Simmer until pasta is tender and soup is thick, stirring occasionally, 20-30 minutes. Add more stock if you wish. Season to taste. Serve with Parmesan cheese.

VARIATIONS   Substitute cannellini (white kidney beans) or mixed beans for chickpeas. Stir in 4-6 cups (1-1.5 L) chopped fresh spinach. Cook about 3 minutes. Garnish each serving with a small spoonful of pesto.

YIELD   **6 SERVINGS**

See photograph on page 51.

GNOCCHI HAM CHOWDER
ITALIAN DUMPLINGS (GNOCCHI) ARE THE MAIN ATTRACTION IN THIS DISH

1 tbsp.	vegetable oil	15 mL
6 oz.	ham, diced	170 g
1 stalk	celery, chopped	1 stalk
1	onion, chopped	1
4 cups	vegetable stock	1 L
1 cup	water	250 mL
2 tbsp.	tomato paste	30 mL
12 oz.	fresh or frozen gnocchi	340 g
3 cups	chopped broccoli florets	750 mL
1 tbsp.	crushed dried basil	15 mL
2 oz.	provolone cheese, shredded	60 g
	salt & pepper to taste	

- In a large heavy soup pot, heat oil. Add ham, celery and onion. Cook until vegetables are tender, about 5 minutes.
- Add stock, water and tomato paste. Bring to a boil. Add gnocchi; return to a boil; reduce heat and simmer for 5 minutes. Add broccoli and simmer for another 10 minutes, or until tender.
- Add basil and cheese; stir until cheese is melted. Season to taste.

YIELD   **6 SERVINGS**

WONTON SOUP

WONTONS:

1 lb.	ground pork	500 g
5 oz.	shrimp, finely chopped	140 g
¼ cup	finely chopped onion	60 mL
½ tsp.	garlic powder	2 mL
¼ tsp.	salt	1 mL
1	egg, separated	1
1 tsp.	soy sauce	5 mL
1 lb.	wonton wrappers	500 g

- In a mixing bowl, combine pork, shrimp, onion, garlic, salt, egg white and soy sauce. Mix well.
- Place 1 tsp. (5 mL) of filling on a corner of each wonton wrapper. Roll that corner over filling and fold in each side, using egg yolk to seal folds. Do not roll up entire wrapper, allow corner opposite pork to extend out.
- Boil wontons in a kettle of boiling water for 5 minutes. Drain well.
- Serve in soup immediately or rinse with cold water, drain and freeze on cookie sheet. Seal frozen wontons in plastic bags.

YIELD   *APPROXIMATELY 72 WONTONS*

WONTON SOUP

2 cups	EACH water & chicken stock	500 mL
2 tbsp.	soy sauce	30 mL
20	wontons	20
1 cup	snow peas	250 mL
¼ cup	chopped green onion	60 mL

- In a saucepan, combine water, stock and soy sauce; bring to a boil. Add wontons. Reduce heat and simmer for 15 minutes.
- Just prior to serving, add snow peas and green onions. Simmer for 2 minutes. Serve immediately.
- This soup may be doubled or tripled according to servings required.

VARIATIONS   Use frozen commercially prepared wontons. Add broccoli florets to the stock; simmer for about 5 minutes.

YIELD   *4 SERVINGS*

PAD THAI SHRIMP SOUP

AN ADAPTATION OF THE WELL-KNOWN THAI STIR-FRY OF THE SAME NAME

4 oz.	rice noodles	115 g
	boiling water	
6 cups	chicken stock	1.5 L
4 oz.	snow peas, halved crosswise	115 g
3 oz.	bean sprouts, halved crosswise	85 g
6 oz.	fresh or cooked shrimp	170 g
3 tbsp.	Thai fish sauce	45 mL
3	green onions, sliced	3
	salt & pepper to taste	

- Place noodles in a bowl. Pour in boiling water to cover; let sit for 10-15 minutes, or until noodles are soft and tender. Drain. Cut noodles into 1" (2.5 cm) lengths.
- In a saucepan, bring stock to a boil. Add snow peas and sprouts. Reduce heat; simmer for 2-3 minutes. Add noodles, shrimp and fish sauce; reheat. Remove from heat; add onions.
- Season to taste; serve hot.

YIELD   *4 SERVINGS*

Thai fish sauce (*nam pla*), Vietnamese (*nuoc nam*), Philippine (*patis*) and Japanese (*shottsuru*) are all pungent, salty and intensely flavorful. Based on the liquid from salted fermented fish, they are used like soy sauce in many dishes. Some are flavored with sugar and some with chili peppers.

ORIENTAL HOT & SOUR SOUP

AN INTERESTING BLEND OF FLAVORS WITH LOTS OF VEGGIES

1 tbsp.	sesame oil	15 mL
3	garlic cloves, minced	3
6 cups	chicken stock	1.5 L
⅓ cup	red wine vinegar	75 mL
1 tbsp.	soy sauce	15 mL
2 tsp.	hot pepper sauce	10 mL
1 tsp.	Worcestershire sauce	5 mL
½ tsp.	pepper	2 mL
1 cup	chopped cooked chicken, pork OR beef	250 mL
10½ oz.	pkg. firm tofu, cubed	297 g
1	carrot, cut into julienne strips	1
8	fresh mushrooms, sliced	8
3	green onions, cut into julienne strips	3
½ cup	bean sprouts	125 mL
3	leaves bok choy (Chinese cabbage), cut into julienne strips	3
12-15	fresh snow peas	12-15

- In a large saucepan or a Dutch oven, heat sesame oil and sauté garlic. Add remaining ingredients, except bok choy and snow peas. Bring to a boil, reduce heat to a simmer and cook until carrots are tender, about 30 minutes.
- Add bok choy and peas. Cook until vegetables are just tender, about 5 minutes.

VARIATIONS A small can of flaked chicken can be substituted for the cooked meat. Beef stock can be substituted for the chicken stock.

YIELD *6 SERVINGS*

HOT SHRIMP SOUP WITH PEPPERS

PEPPERS ADD LIVELY COLOR AND FRESH ZESTY FLAVOR

2 tbsp.	olive oil	30 mL
1	large onion, chopped	1
4	garlic cloves, minced	4
1	red pepper, chopped	1
1	green pepper, chopped	1
1	yellow pepper, chopped	1
1	jalapeño pepper, finely chopped	1
28 oz.	can Italian-style peeled tomatoes, chopped	796 mL
3 cups	chicken stock	750 mL
19 oz.	can black beans, drained, rinsed	540 mL
½ tsp.	hot pepper sauce (optional)	2 mL
8 oz.	bite-sized, cooked, fresh shrimp	250 g
2 tbsp.	fresh lime juice	30 mL
¼ tsp.	ground coriander OR 1 tsp. (5 mL) chopped fresh cilantro	1 mL
	grated Cheddar cheese for garnish	
	chopped green onions for garnish	

- In a large heavy saucepan, heat oil over medium heat.
- Add onion, garlic and peppers. Cook for 5 minutes.
- Add tomatoes, stock, beans and pepper sauce. Bring to a boil; reduce heat and simmer for 20 minutes.
- Add shrimp, lime juice and coriander. Simmer for 2-3 minutes.
- Garnish individual servings with cheese and onions.

YIELD   12 SERVINGS

See photograph on page 69.

HERBED SALMON BISQUE

AROMATIC ROSEMARY IS WONDERFUL WITH SALMON

2 tbsp.	vegetable oil	30 mL
1	onion, chopped	1
½	red OR green pepper, chopped	½
2 stalks	celery, chopped	2 stalks
2	carrots, chopped	2
2	potatoes, peeled, diced	2
2 cups	fish stock OR water	500 mL
2 cups	milk	500 mL
14 oz.	can creamed corn	398 mL
8 oz.	cooked salmon, flaked	250 g
½ tsp.	salt	2 mL
¼ tsp.	pepper	1 mL
2 tsp.	dried parsley	10 mL
1 tsp.	dried rosemary	5 mL

- In a Dutch oven, heat oil; sauté onion, pepper, celery, carrots and potatoes until slightly tender.
- Add stock and bring to a boil. Reduce heat and simmer for 15 minutes.
- Stir in the milk, corn, salmon, salt and pepper. Continue to simmer until vegetables are tender.
- Add parsley and rosemary; simmer for 2 minutes.

VARIATION   Substitute other fish or seafood for the salmon.

YIELD   *6 – 8 SERVINGS*

 Salmon, long prized for its succulent flavor, rich color and silky texture, is now highly recommended as an excellent source of Omega-3 fatty acids. It is also a good source of protein, the B vitamins and vitamin A.

FISH CHOWDER

A HEARTY, TASTY SOUP — EVERY MARITIME KITCHEN HAS A DIFFERENT VERSION

1½ lbs.	white fish fillets, firm-fleshed	750 g
2 tbsp.	butter	30 mL
1 cup	chopped onion	250 mL
½ cup	diced celery	125 mL
3 cups	diced raw potatoes	750 mL
1 cup	sliced carrots	250 mL
3 cups	boiling water	750 mL
1 tsp.	salt	5 mL
¼ tsp.	pepper	1 mL
2 cups	milk	500 mL
	chopped green onions OR parsley for garnish	

- Cut fish fillets into bite-sized pieces.
- In a large heavy saucepan, melt butter. Sauté onion and celery in butter until limp.
- Add potatoes, carrots, water, salt and pepper. Simmer until vegetables are tender, about 25 minutes.
- Add fish. Cook for another 10 minutes, or until fish is cooked.
- Add milk. Reheat but do NOT boil.
- To serve, garnish with chopped green onions or parsley.

YIELD   6 SERVINGS

Salt water fish like cod, haddock, snapper, grouper and halibut are traditional in fish chowders. Monkfish is also delicious. Fresh water fish like pickerel, northern pike and bass make excellent chowders. Oily fish such as mackerel, salmon, tuna, or trout are not traditionally used in chowders.

OYSTER STEW

PURE LUXURY – THIS IS OFTEN SERVED AS AN EAST COAST
THANKSGIVING, CHRISTMAS OR NEW YEAR'S TREAT

2 cups	shucked oysters, liquor reserved	500 mL
¼ cup	butter	60 mL
2 tbsp.	flour	30 mL
2 cups	milk, scalded	500 mL
2 cups	half 'n' half (cereal) cream	500 mL
	salt to taste	
⅛ tsp.	cayenne	0.5 mL
2 tsp.	dry sherry OR Pernod OR dry vermouth (optional)	10 mL
	butter for topping	
	paprika OR coarsely ground black pepper for garnish	

- Drain oysters and reserve oyster liquor. Set oysters aside.
- In a large saucepan, melt butter and blend in flour; cook and stir over low heat for 2 minutes; do NOT brown. Remove from heat.
- Stir in milk and cream, blending until smooth. Bring to a boil, stirring constantly. Cook until smooth and slightly thickened, 3-4 minutes. Stir in oyster liquor, cayenne and salt.
- Add oysters and cook for 6-8 minutes, until they plump and just curl at the edges. Do NOT overcook. Stir in sherry.
- Serve hot stew in bowls, adding a dab of butter and a sprinkle of paprika to each bowl.

VARIATIONS   Omit the flour if you prefer a thinner soup.

For **Oyster Stew Florentine**, cook ½ lb. (250 g) spinach. Purée spinach with ½ cup (125 mL) of the cream, in a blender or food processor. Add to soup with the cream.

Replace sherry with fresh lemon juice.

YIELD   **8 SERVINGS**

Hot Shrimp Soup with Peppers, page 65

LOBSTER BISQUE

DELICIOUS, CREAMY AND RICH — FOR SPECIAL OCCASIONS

¼ cup	butter	60 mL
1	medium onion, finely chopped	1
2	garlic cloves, minced	2
1 stalk	celery, finely chopped	1 stalk
1	carrot, coarsely grated	1
¼ cup	flour	60 mL
3 cups	milk	750 mL
2 cups	whipping cream	500 mL
1 tsp.	salt	5 mL
¼ tsp.	pepper	1 mL
1	bay leaf	1
3 tbsp.	tomato paste	45 mL
12 oz.	fresh lobster meat, coarsely chopped	340 g
1 tsp.	lemon juice	5 mL
	cayenne pepper OR paprika for garnish	
	croûtons for garnish	

- In a large heavy saucepan, melt butter over medium heat. Add onion, garlic, celery and carrot; cook for 4 minutes, or until tender.
- Sprinkle flour over vegetables. Stir and cook for 1 minute.
- While continuing to stir, slowly add milk and cream. Cook until thickened.
- Add salt, pepper, bay leaf, tomato paste and lobster meat. Simmer gently for 10 minutes. Do NOT boil. Stir in lemon juice.
- Remove bay leaf. To serve, sprinkle with cayenne, paprika and croûtons.

VARIATIONS   For a less creamy version, Lobster Bisque may also be made substituting 1 cup (250 mL) EACH water, white wine and fish stock for the milk. Replace 1 cup (250 mL) of the cream with ½ cup (125 mL) EACH beef stock and milk.

Add 2 tbsp. (30 mL) dry sherry or brandy with the lobster meat.

YIELD   **6 SERVINGS**

See photograph on page 157

DANISH CRAB & SHRIMP SOUP

SHELLFISH WITH A SUBTLE CURRY FLAVOR

3 cups	fish OR chicken stock	750 mL
1	medium onion, finely chopped	1
3 tbsp.	butter	45 mL
2 tsp.	curry powder	10 mL
¼ cup	flour	60 mL
4 oz.	EACH crab meat & shrimp	115-170 g
1 tbsp.	cream	15 mL
2 tsp.	dry sherry	10 mL
	lemon twists & chopped parsley for garnish	

- Heat stock in a large saucepan.
- In a skillet, melt butter; sauté onions until translucent. Blend in curry powder and flour. Gradually add to stock; stir until thickened.
- Add crab and shrimp. Cook gently for 10-15 minutes to blend flavors.
- Add cream and sherry. Season to taste. Serve with lemon and parsley.

YIELD   4 SERVINGS

CURRIED CRAB & APPLE SOUP

APPLES AND CURRY ADD FALL FLAVORS TO THIS CREAMY SOUP

3 tbsp.	butter	45 mL
1	medium onion, finely chopped	1
2	medium apples, peeled & coarsely chopped	2
3 tbsp.	flour	45 mL
2 tbsp.	curry powder	30 mL
2 qts.	chicken stock	2 L
2	garlic cloves, crushed	2
1 lb.	crab meat, flaked	500 g
1 cup	whipping cream	250 mL
	salt & pepper to taste	

CURRIED CRAB & APPLE SOUP
(CONTINUED)

- In a large soup pot, melt butter over medium heat; add onion and sauté until translucent, about 4 minutes. Add apples, flour and curry; stir and cook for 3-5 minutes.
- Add stock and garlic; simmer gently, covered, for 20-30 minutes. Add crab for the last 10 minutes.
- Stir in cream and cook over low heat until heated through. Season to taste and serve.

YIELD   *8 SERVINGS*

CHEESE & CRAB CHOWDER
A SILKY-TEXTURED TASTY START TO A SPECIAL DINNER!

4 slices	bacon, chopped	4 slices
1	large onion, chopped	1
¼ cup	flour	60 mL
1 tsp.	salt	5 mL
½ tsp.	EACH pepper, dry mustard & paprika	2 mL
2 cups	chicken stock	500 mL
2 cups	milk	500 mL
6 oz.	cooked crab meat	170 g
4 oz.	mozzarella cheese, grated	115 g

- In a large heavy saucepan, cook bacon until just crisp. Drain off all but 1 tbsp. (15 mL) drippings. Add onion; cook until translucent.
- Sprinkle flour, salt, pepper, dry mustard and paprika over bacon-onion mixture. Stir in.
- Stir in chicken stock and milk. Heat but do NOT boil.
- Add crab meat; heat thoroughly.
- Add mozzarella cheese; heat and stir until melted. Serve hot.

YIELD   *4 – 6 SERVINGS*

BOSTON CLAM CHOWDER

A GREAT AFTER-SKIING, SKATING OR ICE FISHING TREAT!

4 slices	bacon, chopped	4 slices
1	medium onion, chopped	1
1 cup	chopped celery	250 mL
10 oz.	can clams	284 mL
3 cups	cubed potatoes	750 mL
2 cups	water	500 mL
1 tsp.	salt	5 mL
½ tsp.	pepper	2 mL
¼ tsp.	thyme	1 mL
2 tbsp.	butter	30 mL
2 tbsp.	flour	30 mL
2 cups	half 'n' half (cereal) cream	500 mL
	nutmeg for garnish (optional)	

- In a large, heavy saucepan, cook bacon until crisp. Pour off all but 1 tbsp. (15 mL) of bacon drippings. Add onion and celery. Sauté until tender.
- Drain clams reserving liquid. Add clam juice, potatoes, water and spices to saucepan. Boil until potatoes are tender.
- Melt butter. Add flour to make a paste. Add cream. Mix well. Add to saucepan and bring to a boil. Add clams and simmer for 10 minutes.
- Serve hot with Cheese Bread, page 188.

VARIATION   For a thinner chowder omit the flour. Add the butter if you want the extra richness and flavor.

YIELD   *6 SERVINGS*

 New England Clam Chowder "white chowder" is the best-known and tends to be the favorite of traditionalists. Thick or thin, chowders tended to be a fisherman's stew, served with hot homemade bread or with crackers sometimes crumbled in. A *chaudiere* is a heavy, three-legged pot used by French fishermen to cook their catch. Chowder may have originated in Quebec or Acadia and then worked its way down the New England states.

Manhattan Clam Chowder

A PLEASING ALTERNATIVE TO BOSTON CLAM CHOWDER

4 slices	bacon, chopped	4 slices
1	large onion, chopped	1
½ cup	chopped celery	125 mL
2 cups	water	500 mL
2 cups	diced potatoes	500 mL
2 tsp.	salt	10 mL
½ tsp.	pepper	2 mL
28 oz.	can tomatoes	796 mL
1	bay leaf	1
2 x 10 oz.	cans of clams	2 x 284 mL

- In a large heavy saucepan, cook bacon. Add onions and celery. Cook until onions are translucent.
- Add remaining ingredients, except for clams. Simmer gently for 1-2 hours, or until vegetables are tender. Add clams for the last 10 minutes of cooking. Remove bay leaf. Serve hot.

VARIATIONS   Add a few drops of hot pepper sauce or use herb and spice or Mexican-flavored canned tomatoes instead of the regular canned tomatoes.

YIELD   *5 SERVINGS*

In 1939 a bill was introduced in Maine making it an offense to put tomatoes into clam chowder! In Manhattan Clam Chowder, tomatoes are substituted for the milk – a heresy to some, a delight to others. Each type of chowder has its passionate defenders.

SPICY SAUSAGE & CLAM SOUP

A HEARTY CLAM SOUP BURSTING WITH FLAVOR

30	small clams	30
2 tbsp.	olive oil	30 mL
1	onion, finely chopped	1
2 stalks	celery, finely chopped	2 stalks
2	carrots, finely chopped	2
2	large garlic cloves, crushed	2
19 oz.	can crushed tomatoes	540 mL
6 cups	bottled clam juice	1.5 L
6 cups	water	1.5 L
1 tsp.	red pepper flakes, or to taste	5 mL
2 lbs.	spicy Italian sausage, chorizo OR kielbasa (Polish sausage), cut into ¼" (6 mm) slices	1 kg
⅓ cup	minced fresh parsley for garnish	
	salt to taste	

- To clean clams, scrub with a stiff brush under cold water. Discard clams with cracked shells or open clams that do not close when pinched shut.
- In a heavy soup pot, heat oil; add onion, celery, carrots and garlic; cook over medium-low heat, stirring, until vegetables are tender.
- Stir in tomatoes, clam juice, water and red pepper flakes; simmer, covered, for 3 minutes.
- In a heavy skillet brown sausage in batches over moderate heat. Drain on paper towels.
- Add sausage and clams to soup and cook, covered, for 3-6 minutes. Discard any unopened clams. Stir in parsley and salt to taste.

VARIATIONS   Use 10 oz. (284 mL) can of clams instead of fresh clams.
Add a 19 oz. (540 mL) can of chickpeas, drained.
Replace 1-2 cups (250-500 mL) of the water with white wine.
Sauté 1 cup (250 mL) sliced mushrooms with the onions.

YIELD   *6 – 8 SERVINGS*

CIOPPINO

SERVE THIS SUBSTANTIAL ITALIAN-INSPIRED SHELLFISH SOUP WITH CRUSTY
FRENCH BREAD FOR SOAKING UP THE DELICIOUS JUICES

16	EACH clams & mussels in shells	16
2 tbsp.	olive oil	30 mL
1	large onion, chopped	1
1 cup	diced red OR green peppers	250 mL
3-4	garlic cloves, crushed	3-4
28 oz.	canned diced tomatoes	796 mL
	salt, freshly ground pepper & red pepper flakes to taste	
1 tsp.	EACH dried oregano, basil & thyme	5 mL
2 cups	fish stock OR clam juice	500 mL
1 cup	dry white wine	250 mL
1 lb.	firm-fleshed white fish fillets, halibut, red snapper, sea bass, etc, cut into 1" (2.5 cm) cubes	500 g
8-16	large peeled shrimp	8-16
1 lb.	scallops, halved or quartered if large	500 g
1 cup	chopped fresh parsley	250 mL

- Scrub clams and mussels – see instructions on previous page. Set aside.
- In a large soup pot, heat oil; add onion, peppers and garlic. Cook until onions are translucent, not browned.
- Add tomatoes, salt, pepper, pepper flakes, herbs, stock and wine; cover and cook over low heat for 15-20 minutes, until vegetables are tender.
- Add fish and simmer for about 5 minutes. Add shrimp, scallops, clams and mussels. Cover and simmer for about 4-5 minutes, until scallops are opaque and clams and mussels open. Discard any unopened clams or mussels. Stir in parsley and remove from heat.
- Serve in shallow soup bowls.

YIELD   *8 – 10 SERVINGS*

See photograph on front cover.

BOUILLABAISSE

THIS CLASSIC SEAFOOD SOUP FROM THE FRENCH RIVIERA HAS MANY VARIATIONS — USE WHATEVER SHELLFISH AND FISH ARE AVAILABLE

½ cup	olive oil	125 mL
1½ cups	coarsely chopped leeks, white part only	750 mL
1 cup	finely chopped onion	250 mL
3-4	garlic cloves, crushed	3-4
1 cup	tomato paste	250 mL
28 oz.	can diced tomatoes	796 mL
2 tsp.	dried thyme	
½ cup	chopped parsley	125 mL
2	bay leaves	2
2 cups	dry white wine	500 mL
4 cups	fish stock	1 L
	salt & freshly ground pepper to taste	
1½ tsp.	saffron threads	7 mL
24	mussels, scrubbed & cleaned	24
48	clams, scrubbed & cleaned	48
3 lbs.	skinless firm whitefish (bass, snapper, cod, monkfish), cubed	
36	raw shrimp, shelled	36
2-3	1 lb. (500 g) lobster tails, fresh or defrosted, shelled & quartered	2-3
1 tbsp.	Pernod (optional)	15 mL
	chopped fresh parsley for garnish	
	garlic croûtons for garnish	

- In a large soup pot, heat oil; add leeks and onion; cook over medium heat, covered, until tender, about 20 minutes.
- Add garlic to soup pot; sauté for 2-3 minutes. Add tomato paste, tomatoes, thyme, parsley, bay leaves, wine, fish stock, salt and pepper. Simmer for 20 minutes. (Soup can be prepared ahead to this point.)
- Add saffron, mussels and clams in their shells; simmer for 5 minutes. Add fish, shrimp and lobster; simmer for another 5 minutes, until fish is done. Do NOT overcook. Discard unopened mussels and clams.
- Stir in Pernod, if using.

BOUILLABAISSE
(CONTINUED)

- Serve in shallow soup plates. Garnish each serving with parsley and garlic croûtons.

VARIATION   The Spanish soup, ***Zarzuela***, is similar, but add 1 large, finely chopped red pepper and ¼ cup (60 mL) finely chopped serrano ham or prosciutto when you sauté the leeks and onion.

YIELD   **10 SERVINGS**

CHICKEN KALE SOUP
NUTRITIOUS KALE IS POPULAR IN NORTHERN EUROPEAN CUISINE

1 tbsp.	olive oil	15 mL
½ tsp.	red pepper flakes	2 mL
1	bay leaf, crushed	1
½	medium onion, chopped	½
2	garlic cloves, minced	2
1	chicken breast, cubed	1
2	medium potatoes, peeled, cubed	2
6 cups	chicken stock	1.5 L
6-8 cups	lightly packed, shredded kale	1.5-2 L
2-3 tbsp.	lemon juice OR vinegar	30-45 mL
	salt & pepper to taste	

- In a heavy stockpot, heat oil. Add pepper flakes, bay leaf, onion, garlic and chicken. Sauté until onion is translucent and chicken is browned.
- Add potatoes and stock. Bring to a boil; turn down heat and cook until potatoes are tender. Add kale, lemon juice, salt and pepper. Cook briefly, just until kale is tender. Adjust seasonings.

VARIATION   Substitute sorrel, spinach, swiss chard, or beet leaves for the kale.

YIELD   **6 SERVINGS**

CHICKEN & CHICKPEA SOUP

THE SAFFRON ADDS A LOVELY AROMA AND FLAVOR
TO THIS SIMPLE SPANISH-STYLE SOUP

28 oz.	can chickpeas, drained	796 mL
3 lbs.	boneless chicken breasts, cut into 1" (2.5 cm) cubes	1.5 kg
6 cups	chicken stock	1.5 L
28 oz.	can tomatoes	796 mL
¼ cup	tomato paste	60 mL
2 tbsp.	vegetable oil	30 mL
2	garlic cloves, crushed	2
1 cup	chopped onion	250 mL
1 cup	chopped red OR green pepper	250 mL
1 tsp.	red pepper flakes (optional)	5 mL
1 tsp.	salt, or more to taste	5 mL
1-2 pinches	saffron threads	1-2 pinches
	garlic croûtons for garnish	

- In a large heavy soup pot, combine chickpeas, chicken and stock. Bring to a boil and boil for 10 minutes. Reduce heat; cover and simmer until chicken is tender, 30-40 minutes.
- Stir in tomatoes and tomato paste.
- In a small skillet, heat oil; sauté garlic, onion and peppers until onion is translucent. Add to the soup pot. Stir in pepper flakes, salt and saffron. Bring to a boil. Reduce heat and simmer for 15 minutes.
- To serve, ladle into soup bowls and sprinkle with croûtons.

VARIATION Add mussels or clams in their shells or raw shrimp to this soup and cook for about 6-8 minutes. Do NOT overcook. Discard any unopened mussels or clams.

YIELD **8 – 10 SERVINGS**

Senegalese Chicken Peanut Soup

SPICY HOT WITH LOTS OF CURRY AND CAYENNE – ADJUST HEAT TO YOUR TASTE

¼ cup	vegetable oil	60 mL
1	large onion, diced	1
2	garlic cloves, minced	2
6 tbsp.	curry powder, or to taste	90 mL
1-2 tsp.	red pepper flakes	5-10 mL
2 tsp.	ground coriander	10 mL
6 cups	chicken stock	1.5 L
19 oz.	can crushed tomatoes	540 mL
5½ oz.	can tomato paste	156 mL
	salt & pepper to taste	
½ cup	smooth peanut butter	125 mL
1 lb.	cooked chicken breasts, diced	500 g
½ cup	thinly sliced green onion	125 mL
	chopped peanuts & chopped cilantro	
	OR green onions for garnish	

- Heat oil in a large soup pot; add onions and sauté until translucent. Add garlic and cook for 2 minutes. Add curry, pepper flakes and coriander; cook, stirring constantly, 2 more minutes. Add more oil if it is too dry.
- Stir in chicken stock, tomatoes and tomato paste. Simmer for 30 minutes; do NOT boil. Stir often to avoid sticking. Add more stock for desired consistency, if necessary. Add salt and pepper.
- In a blender or food processor, blend peanut butter with 2-3 cups (500-750 mL) of soup, adding stock if too thick. Return blended soup to pot and stir well. Stir in diced chicken. Cook for about 15 minutes. Add green onions; cook for 5 more minutes.
- Garnish individual servings with peanuts and cilantro.

VARIATION   Garnish with garlic croûtons, see page 19.

YIELD   **6 SERVINGS**

See photograph on page 87.

MULLIGATAWNY SOUP

THIS FAMOUS "PEPPER WATER" SOUP IS A SPICY CLASSIC. THE BRITISH
STATIONED IN INDIA POPULARIZED IT THROUGHOUT THE COMMONWEALTH

¼ cup	butter	60 mL
4 lbs.	boneless chicken breasts & thighs, cut into bite-sized pieces	2 kg
3	garlic cloves, crushed	3
1 tsp.	ground cumin, or more to taste	5 mL
½ tsp.	cloves	2 mL
½ tsp.	cinnamon OR nutmeg	2 mL
2-3 tbsp.	curry powder, or to taste	30-45 mL
½ tsp.	ground ginger, or more to taste	2 mL
¼ tsp.	cayenne pepper, or more to taste	1 mL
3 stalks	celery, with leaves, thinly sliced	3 stalks
2	large onions, chopped	2
2	carrots, diced	2
1	leek, white part only, thinly sliced	1
3 qts.	chicken stock	3 L
	salt & freshly ground pepper to taste	
⅔ cup	long-grain rice	150 mL
2 cups	chopped tomatoes (optional)	500 mL
2	tart medium apples, peeled & diced	2
1 cup	plain yogurt	250 mL
2 tbsp.	fresh lemon juice, or to taste	30 mL
½ cup	whipping cream, warmed (optional)	125 mL
	chopped fresh parsley OR cilantro for garnish	
	toasted chopped almonds or peanuts for garnish	

- In a large heavy soup pot, melt butter over medium-high heat. Add chicken and sauté until lightly browned.
- Stir in garlic, cumin, cloves, cinnamon, curry powder, ginger, cayenne, celery, onion, carrots and leek; cook for 2-3 minutes, until aromatic.
- Add stock; simmer, covered, until vegetables are tender, 30-40 minutes.
- Add salt and pepper to taste. Add rice; cover and cook for 15 minutes.
- Stir in tomatoes, apples and yogurt. Simmer for 10 minutes.

MULLIGATAWNY SOUP

(CONTINUED)

- Stir in lemon juice, then cream, if using. Adjust seasonings.
- Sprinkle individual servings with parsley and almonds.

VARIATIONS   Add 1 cup (250 mL) of raisins with the apples.
Substitute turkey breast for the chicken.

YIELD   **10 – 12 SERVINGS**

TURKEY SOUP

GRANDMA'S BOXING DAY SPECIAL!

6 cups	turkey stock	1.5 L
2 cups	cooked diced turkey	500 mL
1	onion, chopped	1
1	garlic clove, minced	1
¼ cup	chopped celery	60 mL
2	medium carrots, diced	2
½ tsp.	salt	2 mL
½ tsp.	pepper	2 mL
2 tbsp.	chopped parsley	30 mL
1	bay leaf	1
1	potato, peeled & diced	1
1 cup	whipping cream	250 mL

- Place all ingredients, except cream, in a large soup kettle. Simmer for 1-2 hours, or until vegetables are tender. Remove bay leaf.
- Stir in cream. Heat thoroughly. Serve hot.

VARIATIONS   Various vegetables may be added in bite-sized pieces. Rice, pearl barley or small-sized pasta may be added if desired. Add additional stock to obtain desired consistency.

YIELD   **6 SERVINGS**

TURKEY BARLEY SOUP

AN UPDATED SCOTCH BROTH – A GREAT WINTER SOUP

1 tbsp.	EACH butter & olive oil	15 mL
1 stalk	celery, chopped	1 stalk
1	medium onion, chopped	1
6 cups	turkey stock	1.5 L
½ cup	pearl barley	125 mL
1	carrot, diced	1
1	potato, peeled, cubed	1
1½ cups	cooked diced turkey	375 mL
½ tsp.	salt	2 mL
¼ tsp.	pepper	1 mL
2	bay leaves	2
½ cup	frozen peas	125 mL
1-2 cups	milk	250-500 mL

- In a heavy stockpot, heat butter and oil; sauté celery and onion until tender.
- Add stock, barley, carrot, potato, turkey, salt, pepper and bay leaves. Simmer gently until barley is tender, about 45 minutes.
- Add frozen peas; simmer for 5 minutes.
- Just prior to serving, add milk to obtain desired consistency. Remove bay leaves.

YIELD   6 SERVINGS

Featuring a nutty roasted flavor, barley has been used since 7,000 B.C. in soups, breads and cereals. It is also used to make beer and Scotch whisky. Pearl barley has the husk, bran and germ removed. It keeps for about 6 months in an airtight container and cooks in about 45 minutes. Pot (Scotch) barley is soaked overnight, drained, then cooked for 1-1½ hours in 4-5 times the volume of liquid.

SOUTH-OF-THE-BORDER TURKEY SOUP

A TASTY, SPICY MEAL IN A BOWL

1 tbsp.	EACH vegetable oil & butter	15 mL
1	onion, chopped	1
1¼ lbs.	ground turkey OR chicken	575 g
1	jalapeño pepper, seeded, finely chopped	1
½	EACH green & red pepper, chopped	½
1 tbsp.	taco seasoning, see page 95	15 mL
2	plum tomatoes, chopped	2
1½ cups	corn kernels	375 mL
6 cups	chicken stock	1.5 L
	freshly grated pepper & salt to taste	
	sour cream, fresh parsley, grated	
	Monterey Jack cheese, crushed corn	
	tortilla chips for garnish	

- In a large heavy stockpot, heat oil and butter over medium heat. Add onion; cook until translucent. Add turkey; sauté until no longer pink.
- Add peppers and taco seasoning; sauté until peppers are tender.
- Add tomatoes, corn, chicken stock and pepper. Bring to a boil; reduce heat. Simmer for 45-60 minutes. Add salt to taste.
- Serve hot and garnish individual servings.

YIELD   **8 SERVINGS**

From the New World to Europe in the 1500s and back again, turkey has been a festive tradition for centuries. High in protein and low in fat, turkey is a good source of iron, zinc, phosphorus, potassium, selenium and B vitamins, including niacin.

Yes, there is a reason why you feel sleepy after a turkey dinner. An amino acid in turkey (tryptophan) helps to produce serotonin. Serotonin has a calming, relaxing effect which may result in a post-turkey indulgence nap!

CABBAGE SOUP

FOR A FULL MEAL, SERVE WITH A CORNED BEEF ON RYE SANDWICH

1 tbsp.	cooking oil	15 mL
½ lb.	lean boneless pork, cubed	250 g
1	medium onion, chopped	1
2	garlic cloves, minced	2
2 stalks	celery, chopped	2 stalks
2½ cups	beef stock	625 mL
14 oz.	can tomato sauce	398 mL
1	small cabbage, shredded	1
1	bay leaf	1
½ tsp.	salt	2 mL
¼ tsp.	pepper	1 mL
½ tsp.	paprika	2 mL
	sour cream (optional)	

- In a Dutch oven, heat cooking oil and brown the pork. Add onion, garlic and celery. Cook until vegetables are just tender.
- Add beef stock to pork, along with remaining ingredients, except sour cream. Bring the soup to a boil.
- Reduce heat, simmer and continue to cook for 1 hour, or until meat is tender. Remove bay leaf.
- Serve garnished with a dollop of sour cream, if desired.

YIELD   **5 – 6 SERVINGS**

 Cabbage is related to broccoli, cauliflower, kale and Brussels sprouts. A cruciferous vegetable, it has been shown to help reduce the incidence of breast and colon cancers. Grown in ancient Greece and Rome, cabbage has long been used as a food and as a medicine. Choose firm, heavy, red or green cabbages free of blemishes. Don't buy halved or shredded cabbage as it starts to lose its vitamin C content when cut. Red or green cabbage will keep up to 2 weeks refrigerated; Savoy cabbage for 1 week.

Senegalese Chicken Peanut Soup, page 81
Couscous Chickpea Salad, page 159

CABBAGE & POTATO SOUP

½ lb.	lean ground pork	250 g
1	onion, diced	1
2	garlic cloves, minced	2
2 cups	packed, shredded cabbage	500 mL
2	tomatoes, diced	2
1	large potato, diced	1
5 cups	chicken stock	1.25 L
1	bay leaf	1
1 tbsp.	chopped fresh dillweed	15 mL
½ tsp.	paprika	2 mL
	salt & pepper to taste	

- In a large soup pot, over medium heat, brown pork; drain off fat.
- Add onion and garlic; sauté for 5 minutes. Add cabbage; sauté for 2 minutes. Add tomatoes; sauté for 2 minutes.
- Add potato, stock and seasonings. Simmer gently for 30 minutes.

YIELD   *6 – 7 SERVINGS*

SPLIT-PEA SOUP

QUEBEC'S HABITANT PEA SOUP – THE BEST USE FOR A HAM BONE!

1	ham bone	1
8 cups	water	2 L
1-2 tsp.	salt (depending on ham)	5-10 mL
1 tsp.	coarse black pepper	5 mL
1	EACH bay leaf & minced garlic clove	1
2 cups	chopped onion	500 mL
1 cup	EACH chopped celery & grated carrot	250 mL
1½ cups	split peas (yellow)	375 mL

- In a large soup pot, place ham bone, water, salt, pepper and bay leaf. Bring to a boil, cover, reduce heat, and simmer for 2 hours.
- Take bone out; remove meat from bone. Return meat to pot.
- Add remaining ingredients. Cover; simmer for 2 hours, until peas are soft.

YIELD   *6 – 8 SERVINGS*

BLACK BEAN SOUP

THIS THICK HEARTY SOUP FROM THE CARIBBEAN IS VERY POPULAR

1 cup	dry black beans	250 mL
5 cups	water	1.25 L
4 slices	bacon, chopped	4 slices
1	EACH onion, carrot, celery stalk, chopped	1
2-3	garlic cloves, minced	2-3
1	red OR green pepper, chopped	1
½ cup	chili sauce	125 mL
19 oz.	can diced tomatoes (optional)	540 mL
1	bay leaf	1
1 tsp.	ground cumin, or more to taste	5 mL
1½ tsp.	salt	7 mL
½ tsp.	EACH black pepper & cayenne	2 mL
1½ tsp.	vinegar	7 mL
2 tbsp.	chopped pimiento	30 mL
2 tbsp.	sherry OR fresh lime juice	30 mL
	chicken stock	
	chopped green onion & chopped hard-boiled egg for garnish	

- Soak beans in water overnight. Drain. In a large saucepan, cover beans with fresh water and cook for 1½-2 hours, or until tender.
- In a skillet over medium heat, cook bacon with onion, carrot, celery, garlic and red pepper, until vegetables begin to soften. Add to beans.
- Add chili sauce, tomatoes, bay leaf, cumin, salt, black pepper and cayenne pepper. Cover and simmer for 2-3 hours.
- Add vinegar, pimiento and sherry. Cook for 30 minutes more to blend flavors. Remove bay leaf. Mash beans slightly.
- If necessary, add chicken stock for desired consistency.
- Serve garnished with chopped green onion and chopped egg.

VARIATIONS   Add 1 tbsp. (15 mL) dried oregano. You may substitute a 19 oz. (540 mL) can of black beans for the dried beans and omit the first step. Try a dollop of sour cream for garnish. Also try chopped tomatoes, green peppers, onions and grated Cheddar cheese as garnishes. Add ½ lb. (250 g) of small shrimp or flaked crab meat to the soup just before serving. Heat through.

YIELD   *4 – 6 SERVINGS*

CAJUN BEAN SOUP

HEARTY AND WHOLESOME – SPICE IT TO TASTE

1 tbsp.	vegetable oil	15 mL
3 slices	bacon, chopped	3 slices
1	medium onion, chopped	1
2 stalks	celery, chopped	2 stalks
½	red chili pepper, finely chopped	½
2	garlic cloves, minced	2
28 oz.	can stewed tomatoes	796 mL
2 cups	vegetable stock	500 mL
2	bay leaves	2
½ tsp.	salt	2 mL
14 oz.	can pinto beans, drained, rinsed	398 mL

- In a heavy-bottomed saucepan, heat oil. Add bacon; cook until crisp. Drain off all but 1 tbsp. (15 mL) of drippings.
- Add onion, celery, pepper and garlic. Cook until onion is translucent.
- Add remaining ingredients. Bring to a boil, reduce heat, simmer for 30 minutes.

VARIATIONS   Substitute a can of mixed beans for the pinto beans.

Substitute hot pepper sauce OR cayenne to taste for the red chili pepper.

YIELD   **6 SERVINGS**

Cajun (French Canadian/Acadian) recipes tend to be hearty, peppery, one-dish "country" food. Each family has their own version of favorite recipes, passed down from mother to daughter (or father to son). Their recipes are always changing as they add available/seasonal fish, wild game and vegetables. Cayenne and hot pepper sauces are the usual sources of "heat".

LENTIL SAUSAGE POTAGE

THICK AND GARLICKY – A FULL-BODIED SOUP –
PERFECT AFTER A DAY OF SKIING OR SNOWMOBILING

1 tbsp.	vegetable oil	15 mL
4 slices	smoked maple ham OR bacon, chopped	4 slices
1	onion, chopped	1
½	green pepper, chopped	½
2	garlic cloves, crushed	2
1	carrot, chopped	1
1 stalk	celery, chopped	1 stalk
2 qts.	beef stock	2 L
1 cup	lentils, rinsed in cold water	250 mL
2	bay leaves	2
¼ tsp.	ground thyme	1 mL
1 cup	instant potato flakes	250 mL
1 tbsp.	apple cider vinegar	15 mL
	salt & pepper to taste	
½	ring of garlic or ham sausage, coarsely chopped	½

- In a Dutch oven, heat oil. Sauté ham, onion, green pepper, garlic, carrot and celery, until vegetables are just tender.
- Add stock, lentils, bay leaves and thyme. Bring soup to a boil.
- Reduce heat; simmer for 30 minutes, or until lentils are tender. Remove bay leaves.
- Add remaining ingredients; cook an additional few minutes until soup is thickened and sausage is thoroughly heated.

NOTE   Potato flakes are used to thicken the soup. If you prefer, shake 2-3 tbsp. (30-45 mL) of flour in ½ cup (125 mL) of water until smooth. Stir into soup to thicken.

YIELD   *6 – 8 SERVINGS*

BEEF GOULASH SOUP

HUNGARIAN PAPRIKA ADDS SPICY SWEETNESS

2 cups	beef stock	500 mL
1 cup	water	250 mL
2 cups	chopped cooked beef	500 mL
2	potatoes, peeled, cubed	2
1	medium onion, chopped	1
2	garlic cloves, minced	2
1 tsp.	dried thyme	5 mL
8 oz.	can tomato sauce	250 mL
2 tbsp.	red wine vinegar	30 mL
2 tsp.	Worcestershire sauce	10 mL
¼ cup	flour	60 mL
2 tbsp.	Hungarian paprika	30 mL
½ cup	water	125 mL
1 cup	frozen peas	250 mL
	salt & pepper to taste	

- In a large saucepan, combine stock, 1 cup (250 mL) water, beef, potatoes, onion, garlic, thyme, tomato sauce, vinegar and Worcestershire sauce. Bring to a gentle boil and cook until vegetables are tender.
- In a small bowl, combine flour, Hungarian paprika and water.
- Add peas to goulash. Bring to a quick boil. Add the flour mixture, stirring until thickened and bubbly. Cook for an additional 2 minutes.
- Season with salt and pepper.

VARIATION   For **Hungarian Goulash**, use half of the stock and omit the water. Serve over noodles with a dollop of sour cream.

YIELD   *4 – 6 SERVINGS*

 Paprika, made of ground dried ripe sweet peppers, varies in color and flavor, from orange to dark red, from mild to fiery. Hungarian paprika, an essential part of Hungarian cuisine, is considered to be the best. It is available in both hot and mild versions.

HAMBURGER SOUP

ITS LASTING POPULARITY SPEAKS FOR ITSELF

1 tbsp.	vegetable oil	15 mL
1 lb.	lean ground beef	500 g
1	medium onion, chopped	1
4 cups	beef stock	1 L
28 oz.	can tomatoes	796 mL
4	potatoes, peeled & diced	4
4	carrots, chopped	4
3 stalks	celery, chopped	3 stalks
1 cup	shredded cabbage	250 mL
14 oz.	can tomato sauce	398 mL
1	bay leaf	1
¼ tsp.	thyme	1 mL
¼ tsp.	basil	1 mL
1 tsp.	salt	5 mL
½ tsp.	pepper	2 mL

- In a skillet, heat oil and brown the beef. Drain off fat. Add onions and continue to sauté until onions are translucent. Transfer to a Dutch oven or a slow cooker.
- Add beef stock to the beef mixture.
- Add remaining ingredients. Cover and cook slowly for 1-2 hours, or until vegetables are tender.
- If desired, extra liquid may be added to obtain desired consistency.

VARIATION   To extend this soup or to vary it, add ½-1 cup (125-250 mL) of small pasta shells or noodles.

YIELD   **6 – 8 SERVINGS**

 For lower-fat soups and stews, rinse browned ground beef in a colander to eliminate as much fat as possible. Return beef to pan and proceed with the soup. No flavor is lost.

TACO SOUP

A COUSIN TO CHILI CON CARNE – AND EVERY BIT AS DELICIOUS

1 tbsp.	vegetable oil	15 mL
1 lb.	lean ground beef	500 g
1	medium onion, chopped	1
2	garlic cloves, minced	2
1 tbsp.	taco seasoning (see recipe below)	15 mL
19 oz.	can kidney beans, undrained	540 mL
12 oz.	can kernel corn, undrained	341 mL
28 oz.	can stewed tomatoes	796 mL
1	green pepper, chopped (optional)	1
5½ oz.	can tomato paste	156 mL
	sour cream	
	grated Cheddar cheese	
	tortilla chips	

- In a Dutch oven, heat oil; brown the beef. Drain off fat. Add onion and garlic and cook until onions are translucent.
- Add taco seasoning, beans, corn, tomatoes, green pepper and tomato paste. Simmer slowly, stirring occasionally, for 2 hours.
- Add water to obtain desired consistency.
- Serve garnished with sour cream and Cheddar cheese. Tortilla chips can be served on the side or crumbled into the soup.

YIELD   *5 – 6 SERVINGS*

TACO SEASONING MIX

½ cup	salt	125 mL
½ cup	chili powder	125 mL
¼ cup	crushed, dried red chili peppers	60 mL
¼ cup	instant minced garlic	60 mL
2 tbsp.	ground oregano	30 mL
¼ cup	cumin	60 mL

- Combine all ingredients. Store in a cool place. Use as required.

BEEF 'N' BEAN SOUP

2 tbsp.	vegetable oil	30 mL
1 lb.	lean ground beef	500 g
1	medium onion, chopped	1
2	garlic cloves, minced	2
2 stalks	celery, chopped	2 stalks
1	green pepper, chopped	1
19 oz.	can Romano beans, drained	540 mL
4 cups	beef stock	1 L
2	large tomatoes, chopped	2
	salt & pepper to taste	
1 tsp.	dried crushed oregano	5 mL

- In a Dutch oven, heat oil; brown ground beef. Drain off fat.
- Add onion, garlic, celery and pepper; cook until onions are translucent.
- Add beans, stock, tomatoes, salt, pepper and oregano; bring to a boil. Reduce heat; cover and simmer for 30 minutes.

YIELD   *6 SERVINGS*

HEARTY HUNTER'S SOUP

ALSO TRY THIS COUNTRY SOUP WITH ELK, VENISON OR CARIBOU

2 tbsp.	vegetable oil	30 mL
1 lb.	ground moose meat OR ground beef	500 g
1	medium onion, chopped	1
2 stalks	celery, chopped	2 stalks
2	garlic cloves, minced	2
4 cups	beef stock	1 L
28 oz.	can tomatoes	796 mL
14 oz.	can tomato sauce	398 mL
4	carrots, chopped	4
4	potatoes, cubed	4
2	bay leaves	2
1 tsp.	EACH dried thyme, oregano & basil	5 mL
	salt & pepper to taste	

HEARTY HUNTER'S SOUP

(CONTINUED)

- In a Dutch oven, over medium heat, heat oil and brown meat. Add onion, celery and garlic; sauté until onion is translucent.
- Add remaining ingredients. Bring to a boil. Cover; reduce heat. Cook until vegetables are tender, about 30 minutes. Add extra stock if desired.

VARIATION   Barley, rice or pasta may be added, with vegetables, to extend or vary soup.

YIELD   **8 SERVINGS**

MIDDLE EASTERN VEGETABLE STEW

ALLSPICE ADDS THE SEDUCTIVE FLAVORS OF CINNAMON, NUTMEG AND CLOVES

2 tbsp.	olive oil	30 mL
1	large onion, chopped	1
1	eggplant, diced	1
	salt & pepper to taste	
2	small zucchini, diced	2
2	tomatoes, chopped	2
½ cup	vegetable stock	125 mL
½ tsp.	ground allspice	2 mL
19 oz.	can chickpeas, drained, rinsed	540 mL
	chopped fresh parsley	60 mL

- In a heavy saucepan, heat oil. Add onion; cook until translucent. Add eggplant, salt and pepper; cover and cook over low heat for 5 minutes. Add zucchini and tomatoes; cover and cook an additional 3 minutes.
- Add remaining ingredients. Simmer for 30 minutes, or until eggplant is tender. Add parsley; simmer for 30 seconds.

Variation   For a Provence ratatouille-like stew, add 1 red or green pepper, coarsely diced, 2 garlic cloves, 2 tbsp. (30 mL) EACH chopped fresh basil and oregano. Add with the vegetable stock. Omit allspice and chickpeas.

NOTE   Eggplant and zucchinis do not need to be peeled unless skins are tough.

YIELD   **4 – 6 SERVINGS**

SHRIMP JAMBALAYA

THIS IS ONE OF CREOLE COOKERY'S FINEST!

4 oz.	bacon, chopped	115 g
2	garlic cloves, minced	2
1	onion, chopped	1
1 stalk	celery, chopped	1 stalk
1	green pepper, finely chopped	1
1-2	jalapeño peppers, seeded & finely chopped	1-2
2	bay leaves	2
½ tsp.	dried thyme	2 mL
2 tsp.	parsley flakes	10 mL
14 oz.	can tomatoes	398 mL
5½ oz.	can tomato paste	156 g
½ tsp.	salt	2 mL
¼ tsp.	pepper	1 mL
2 lbs.	cleaned, raw shrimp	1 kg
2 cups	cooked rice	500 mL

- In a large skillet, fry the bacon. Drain off all but 1 tbsp. (15 mL) of drippings. Add garlic, onion, celery and peppers. Cook until onion is tender.
- Add bay leaves, thyme, parsley, tomatoes, tomato paste, salt and pepper. Bring to a boil. Reduce heat and cook slowly for 20-30 minutes.
- Add shrimp and cook for 5 more minutes.
- Add rice. When thoroughly heated, serve.

VARIATION   If desired, scallops may be added, along with the shrimp.

YIELD   *6-8 SERVINGS*

CHICKEN, SAUSAGE & SHRIMP JAMBALAYA

A SENSATIONAL AND VERSATILE CREOLE CLASSIC

3 tbsp.	vegetable OR olive oil	45 mL
2 lbs.	boneless chicken thighs or breasts	1 kg
2 stalks	celery, chopped	2 stalks
1	medium onion, chopped	1
1	green OR red pepper, chopped	1
2-3	garlic cloves, minced	2-3
1 lb.	cooked smoked sausage – andouille OR hot or mild Italian OR kielbasa, cut into ½" (1.3 cm) slices	500 g
2-3 tsp.	Cajun OR Creole seasoning	10-15 mL
2	bay leaves	2
28 oz.	can stewed tomatoes	796 mL
1	lemon	1
1 lb.	cooked, peeled, deveined shrimp	500 g
	salt & pepper to taste	

- In a large skillet, heat oil and sauté chicken in batches until browned, set aside. Add celery, onion, pepper and garlic and sauté until tender, about 5 minutes.
- Reduce heat to a simmer. Add sausage, Cajun seasoning, bay leaf, stewed tomatoes and chicken.
- Slice the lemon; cut slices into quarters. Add to tomato mixture. Simmer for 30 minutes, or until thickened.
- Add shrimp; simmer for about 5 minutes, or until heated through.
- Adjust flavoring with salt and pepper. Serve with cooked rice.

VARIATIONS 2 cups (500 mL) long-grain rice may be stirred into sautéed vegetable mixture. Add 4 cups (1 L) chicken stock with stewed tomatoes.

NOTE For **Cajun** or **Creole Seasoning**, substitute 2 tsp. (10 mL) chili powder and ½ tsp. (2 mL) EACH cayenne pepper, dried thyme and oregano.

YIELD **8 SERVINGS**

CHICKEN WITH EGG NOODLES

ALTHOUGH TIME CONSUMING THIS IS WELL WORTH THE TIME AND EFFORT!

CHICKEN:

1	chicken, cut into serving pieces	1
	water	
½ cup	chopped onion	125 mL
1 tbsp.	parsley	15 mL
1 tsp.	salt	5 mL
½ tsp.	pepper	2 mL
½ cup	chopped celery	125 mL

NOODLES:

4	eggs, beaten	4
2 tbsp.	water	30mL
1 tbsp.	oil	15 mL
3 cups	flour	750 mL
1 tsp.	salt	5 mL

- Place chicken pieces in a large soup pot. Add water until chicken is completely covered. Add remaining ingredients. Simmer for 2 hours or until chicken is well done. (Meanwhile prepare noodles). Remove chicken from stock to a casserole to keep warm. Reserve stock for noodles.
- To prepare noodles, beat eggs, water and oil. Add flour and salt. Knead until flour is blended and dough does not stick to the hands. Cover dough with a bowl and let rest for 30 minutes.
- Roll out pieces of dough on a floured surface until paper thin. Sprinkle flour over each piece and stack sheets of dough. When all dough has been rolled, floured and stacked, cut dough into spaghetti-thin strips. Use adequate flour to ensure that noodles do not stick together.
- Boil chicken stock. Add noodles by handfuls, stirring constantly to prevent noodles from sticking together. Additional boiling water may have to be added at this point to provide enough liquid to cook noodles.
- When all noodles are in the stock, turn heat down to medium. Cook for 15 minutes, stirring frequently. Noodles will thicken stock mixture. Serve immediately with chicken.

YIELD   6 SERVINGS

Coq au Vin

A SIMPLE VERSION OF THE CLASSIC BURGUNDIAN CHICKEN STEW

1 tbsp.	olive oil	15 mL
1 tbsp.	butter	15 mL
2	whole chicken breasts, boneless, skinless, cut into 1" (2.5 cm) square pieces	2
4 slices	bacon, chopped (optional)	4 slices
1	onion, coarsely chopped	1
½	rutabaga OR turnip, diced	½
2	carrots, diced	2
1 cup	chicken stock	250 mL
½ tsp.	salt	2 mL
¼ tsp.	pepper	1 mL
1 tsp.	crushed dried thyme	5 mL
1	bay leaf	1
¾ cup	dry red wine	175 mL
8	mushrooms, quartered	8

- In a large heavy Dutch oven, heat oil and butter. Add chicken pieces and brown. If using bacon, remove chicken from pan; sauté bacon until crisp, drain off most of the fat. Return chicken to pan.
- Add onion, rutabaga, carrot, stock, salt, pepper, thyme and bay leaf. Cover; reduce heat to a simmer. Cook for 30-45 minutes, or until vegetables are just tender.
- Add the wine and mushrooms. Bring to a boil, then reduce heat; cover and simmer for an additional 15-20 minutes.
- Remove bay leaf. Serve hot.

VARIATIONS Substitute chicken thighs for the breasts; add 2 crushed garlic cloves. For a festive occasion, flame browned chicken breasts with about ¼ cup (60 mL) warmed brandy or Calvados.

YIELD **5 – 6 SERVINGS**

CHICKEN CACCIATORE

HUNTER'S-STYLE CHICKEN – EVERY ITALIAN FAMILY HAS A FAVORITE RECIPE

½ cup	flour	125 mL
1 tsp.	salt	5 mL
¼ tsp.	pepper	1 mL
10	chicken thighs, skinned	10
2 tbsp.	butter	30 mL
2 tbsp.	olive OR vegetable oil	30 mL
2	garlic cloves, minced	2
1	large onion, sliced	1
½	green pepper, chopped	½
28 oz.	can Italian-style tomatoes	796 mL
1 tbsp.	dried parsley	15 mL
1 tsp.	dried oregano	5 mL
¼ tsp.	ground thyme	1 mL
2 cups	sliced mushrooms OR 10 oz. (284 mL)	500 mL
	can mushroom stems & pieces, drained	
	salt & pepper to taste	

- In a plastic bag, combine flour, salt and pepper. Add chicken; shake bag to coat chicken pieces.
- In a large skillet, heat butter and oil. Add garlic and sauté briefly.
- Add chicken pieces to pan; brown on all sides.
- Add onion, pepper, tomatoes, parsley, oregano and thyme. Cover tightly; reduce heat to simmer. Cook for 30 minutes, stirring occasionally.
- Add mushrooms, salt and pepper. Continue to simmer for an additional 10 minutes, or until chicken is tender. Serve over rice, noodles or polenta.

VARIATION   Substitute 1½ tsp. (7 mL) EACH chopped fresh rosemary and sage, or ½ tsp. (2 mL) dried, for the parsley, oregano and thyme. Add ½ cup (125 mL) pitted, sliced Italian black olives.

YIELD   ***6 – 8 SERVINGS***

CHICKEN PAPRIKA (*PAPRIKAS CSIRKE*)

THIS TRADITIONAL HUNGARIAN DISH FREES THE COOK
TO ENJOY THE GUESTS

¼ cup	butter OR margarine	60 mL
1	large onion, chopped	1
1	garlic clove, minced	1
1 tbsp.	Hungarian paprika	15 mL
½ tsp.	salt	2 mL
½ tsp.	pepper	2 mL
3 lbs.	chicken pieces	1.5 kg
2 cups	chicken stock	500 mL
2 tsp.	flour	10 mL
1 cup	sour cream	250 mL

- In a large skillet or heavy saucepan, heat butter; sauté onion and garlic until golden brown. Stir in paprika, salt and pepper. Cook for 1 minute.
- Add chicken pieces and fry until lightly browned.
- Stir in stock. Cook over low heat for 1 hour, or until chicken is tender.
- Whisk flour into sour cream. Add to chicken liquid and heat. Do NOT boil.
- Serve with dumplings or noodles.

VARIATIONS   Vegetables such as skinned chopped tomatoes, chopped green peppers or sliced carrots may be added with the stock.

Cheaper, less tender cuts of meat may be substituted for the chicken. Boneless meat should be in small cubes.

YIELD   *5 – 6 SERVINGS*

 Store sour cream and cottage cheese cartons upside down in the refrigerator to double the life of the contents.

CHICKEN & MIXED BEAN CHILI

CHICKEN CHILI – SATISFYING AND VERSATILE

1 tbsp.	olive oil	15 mL
2	skinless, boneless chicken breast halves, diced OR 1 lb. (500 g) ground chicken	2
1	medium onion, chopped	1
1	large carrot, diced (optional)	1
½	red OR green pepper, diced	½
2 stalks	celery, sliced	2 stalks
2	garlic cloves, crushed	2
1 tsp.	cumin	5 mL
2 tbsp.	chili powder	30 mL
¼ tsp.	red pepper flakes	1 mL
19 oz.	can diced tomatoes	540 mL
1 cup	chicken stock	250 mL
19 oz.	can mixed beans, drained	540 mL
2 tsp.	sugar	10 mL
	salt & pepper to taste	

- In a large saucepan, heat oil over medium-high heat. Add chicken; cook until lightly browned.
- Add onion, carrot, peppers, celery and garlic. Cook for 4 minutes, stirring occasionally.
- Add cumin, chili powder, red pepper flakes; cook and stir for 1 minute. Add tomatoes, and stock. Reduce heat to low; cover and simmer for 15 minutes.
- Add beans and sugar. Simmer for 15 minutes, uncovered.
- Serve over rice.

VARIATIONS   *Turkey Chili* – substitute diced or ground turkey breast for the chicken.

Vegetarian Chili – substitute 19 oz. (540 mL) can of chickpeas for the chicken. Add chickpeas with the tomatoes.

YIELD   *4 SERVINGS*

Spinach Apple Salad, page 136
Pork Ragout with Sweet Potatoes & Apricots, page 107
Sour Cream Biscuits, page 181

Pork Ragoût with Sweet Potatoes & Apricots

DOUBLES, TRIPLES AND FREEZES WELL — TENDER, SAVORY AND SWEET

2 tbsp.	Dijon mustard	30 mL
¾ lb.	pork loin boneless chops, trimmed of fat, cubed	340 g
2 tbsp.	brown sugar	30 mL
2 tbsp.	flour	30 mL
½ tsp.	salt	2 mL
¼ tsp.	freshly ground pepper	1 mL
2 tbsp.	vegetable oil	30 mL
½	onion, chopped	½
1	garlic clove, crushed	1
½ cup	chicken stock	125 mL
2	sweet potatoes, peeled & cubed	2
½ cup	halved, dried apricots	125 mL

- Place mustard and cubed pork into a plastic bag; shake to coat pork. Combine sugar, flour, salt and pepper. Add to plastic bag and dredge mustard-covered pork in flour mixture.
- In a Dutch oven, heat oil over medium heat. Brown pork in oil. Add onion and garlic and continue to cook until onion is softened. Stir in chicken stock, scraping up browned bits on bottom of pan. Add sweet potatoes and apricot halves. Combine well.
- Reduce heat to low; cover. Cook, stirring occasionally, for 45 minutes, or until tender.
- Serve over a bed of rice or noodles with a tossed salad or vegetable.

VARIATIONS Substitute apple cider or juice, or even half juice and half beer, for the chicken stock. For a Mediterranean flavor, add ¼ tsp. (1 mL) each ground coriander and cinnamon, plus ¼ cup (60 mL) chopped pitted prunes.

YIELD *6 SERVINGS*

See photograph on page 105.

PORK STEW

RICH AND FLAVORFUL – HUNGARIAN PAPRIKA DOES MAKE A DIFFERENCE
– IT'S WORTH THE SEARCH

1 tbsp.	olive oil	15 mL
1	medium onion, sliced	1
3 tbsp.	Hungarian paprika	45 mL
2	garlic cloves, minced	2
1 lb.	pork tenderloin, cut into 1" (2.5 cm) cubes	500 g
1 tsp.	lemon pepper	5 mL
1 tsp.	salt	5 mL
14 oz.	can plum tomatoes	398 mL
½ cup	tomato juice	125 mL
½ cup	sour cream	125 mL

- In a heavy saucepan, heat oil over medium heat. Add onion; cook until translucent. Add paprika and garlic; cook for 1 minute while stirring.
- Add pork and seasonings. Cook and stir until pork is lightly browned.
- Add tomatoes and tomato juice. Simmer for 30 minutes, or until pork is tender.
- Remove from heat. Stir in sour cream.
- Serve hot over cooked egg noodles, steamed rice or mashed potatoes.

YIELD   *4 – 5 SERVINGS*

Lemon Pepper is a popular seasoning mix. To make your own version, combine ⅓ cup (75 mL) coarsely ground black pepper, 2 tbsp. (30 mL) dried lemon zest, 1 tbsp. (15 mL) crushed coriander seeds, 4 tsp. (20 mL) EACH dried minced onion and thyme. Place in an airtight jar and store in a cool, dark place.

POLISH HUNTER'S STEW (*BIGOS*)

ONE OF THE GREAT PEASANT DISHES OF THE WORLD

1 oz.	dried Polish (*Boletus*) OR porcini mushrooms	30 g
4 cups	sauerkraut, rinsed, drained	1 L
1½ lbs.	pork back ribs	680 g
2	bay leaves	2
20	black peppercorns	20
2	whole allspice berries	2
2-3	garlic cloves, minced	2-3
6 cups	beef stock	1.5 L
½	medium cabbage, finely chopped	½
8 oz.	bacon	225 g
1 tbsp.	butter	15 mL
1	medium onion, chopped	1
10 oz.	Polish smoked sausage (kielbasa), cubed	300 g
	Maggi seasoning to taste	
	salt & pepper to taste	

- Soak dried mushrooms in boiling water for at least 30 minutes; drain.
- In a large stockpot, combine sauerkraut, ribs, bay leaves, peppercorns, allspice berries, garlic and stock. Bring to a boil; reduce heat, cover and simmer for 2 hours, or until ribs are tender. Remove ribs; cool.
- Add cabbage to sauerkraut mixture; simmer until cabbage is tender.
- Remove meat from ribs; cut into ¼" (6 mm) cubes.
- In a skillet, fry bacon until crisp; drain and crumble.
- Melt butter in skillet; sauté onion until translucent.
- Add pork rib meat, sausage, bacon, mushrooms, onion, Maggi, salt and pepper to sauerkraut mixture. Cover; simmer until thoroughly heated, about 30-40 minutes. Discard bay leaves. Serve hot with sour cream, boiled potatoes, rye bread and beer. This is even better the next day.

VARIATIONS	Replace 2 cups (500 mL) of beef stock with dry white or red wine OR use 1 cup (250 mL) EACH white wine and apple cider. Add 8 juniper berries, crushed, or 2 tbsp. (30 mL) gin.
NOTE	Maggi is a basic in European kitchens. Fresh maggi, also known as lovage or sea parsley, has a strong celery flavor and fragrance.
YIELD	*10 SERVINGS*

GROUND BEEF STROGANOFF

A MODERN VERSION OF A CLASSIC DISH

1 tbsp.	vegetable oil	15 mL
1 lb.	lean ground beef	500 g
1	large onion, chopped	1
2	garlic cloves, minced	2
10 oz.	can mushroom pieces, drained	284 mL
2 cups	beef stock	500 mL
1 cup	sour cream	250 mL
2 tbsp.	flour	30 mL

- In a large skillet, heat oil and brown beef. Drain off fat. Add onion, garlic and mushrooms. Sauté until onions are translucent. Stir in beef stock.
- Combine sour cream and flour. Stir into beef mixture. Simmer for approximately 30 minutes, stirring occasionally.
- Serve over egg noodles with a side salad.

YIELD   5 – 6 SERVINGS

CHILI CON CARNE

GREAT TO COME HOME TO AFTER A WINTER DAY OUTDOORS!

2 tbsp.	vegetable oil	30 mL
1½ lbs.	lean ground beef	750 g
1 cup	chopped onion	250 mL
2	garlic cloves, minced	2
2 cups	stewed tomatoes	500 mL
1 cup	tomato sauce	250 mL
1 cup	sliced mushrooms	250 mL
3 x 14 oz.	cans kidney beans	3 x 398 mL
2 tbsp.	chili powder, or more to taste	30 mL
1 tbsp.	hot chili OR pepper sauce	15 mL
1 tsp.	EACH black pepper & dried oregano	5 mL

CHILI CON CARNE

(CONTINUED)

- Heat oil in a large heavy pan; sauté beef, onion and garlic until beef is no longer pink.
- Add remaining ingredients. Simmer for 3 hours, stirring occasionally.
- Serve hot with Pepper Corn Bread, page 185, or baking powder biscuits, pages 181-183.

YIELD   *8 – 10 SERVINGS*

BLACK BEAN CHILI

BLACK BEANS (TURTLE BEANS) HAVE AN EARTHY SWEET FLAVOR

2 tbsp.	olive oil	30 mL
1	medium onion, chopped	1
2	garlic cloves, minced	2
2 stalks	celery, chopped	2 stalks
1	green OR red pepper, diced	1
1 lb.	extra-lean ground beef	500 g
2 x 19 oz.	cans black turtle beans, drained	2 x 540 mL
28 oz.	can Italian-style peeled tomatoes	796 mL
1	jalapeño pepper, minced	1
1-3 tbsp.	chili powder, or more to taste	15-45 mL
	salt & pepper to taste	

- In a large heavy saucepan, over medium-high heat, heat oil; sauté onion, garlic, celery, pepper and beef until beef is no longer pink.
- Add remaining ingredients, reduce heat; simmer for 1-2 hours.

VARIATION   ***Chili Toppings*** add great flavor and color to any chili. Top individual servings with chopped onion, red or green peppers, grated Cheddar cheese and sour cream. Serve toppings in small bowls.

YIELD   *6 – 8 SERVINGS*

CHUNKY CHILI STEW

ADDED VEGETABLES MEAN ADDED FLAVOR AND NUTRITION

6 slices	bacon, diced	6 slices
1 cup	diced onion	250 mL
½	green pepper, diced	½
1	garlic clove, crushed	1
1 lb.	lean ground beef	500 g
1-2 tbsp.	chili powder, or more to taste	15-30 mL
1 tsp.	seasoning salt	5 mL
¼-½ tsp.	red pepper flakes	1-2 mL
19 oz.	can diced tomatoes	540 mL
½ cup	water	125 mL
1 stalk	celery, chopped	1 stalk
2	large carrots, chopped	2
2	medium potatoes, cubed	2
12 oz.	can whole kernel corn	341 mL
14 oz.	can kidney beans, drained	398 mL
14 oz.	can beans in molasses	398 mL

- In a large heavy saucepan, over medium heat, sauté bacon until crisp.
- Remove bacon; sauté onion, green pepper and garlic in bacon drippings until soft.
- Add ground beef; cook until browned, stirring to break up. Drain off excess fat.
- Stir in chili powder, seasoning salt, pepper flakes, tomatoes and water.
- Add celery, carrots and potato; stir; cover and simmer for 30 minutes.
- Add corn, kidney beans and beans in molasses; stir. Cover and simmer for 30 minutes. Stir in crisp bacon.

YIELD   *8 SERVINGS*

HOT TORNADO STEW

GUTSY FLAVOR – BEER, SALSA AND PEPPERS

1 lb.	stewing beef, in ½" (1.3 cm) cubes	500 g
2 tbsp.	vegetable oil	30 mL
1	medium onion, chopped	1
1 stalk	celery, chopped	1 stalk
2	garlic cloves, minced	2
5½ oz.	can tomato paste	156 mL
12 oz.	can vegetable cocktail juice	340 mL
2	canned roasted red peppers, chopped	2
12 oz.	beer (1 bottle)	340 mL
¼ cup	salsa	60 mL
½ tsp.	cayenne pepper	2 mL
½ tsp.	salt	2 mL
1 tsp.	chili powder	5 mL
¼ tsp.	celery seed	1 mL
¼ tsp.	hot pepper sauce (optional)	1 mL
4	potatoes, peeled, cubed	4

- In a large heavy pan, over medium heat, heat oil and brown meat. Add onion, celery and garlic; cook for 3 minutes.
- Add remaining ingredients. Lower heat; simmer, stirring occasionally, for 2 hours, or until meat and potatoes are tender.

YIELD   *4 – 5 SERVINGS*

For basting or for marinades, beer is a wonderful flavoring option. It adds subtle flavor to meats, shellfish, vegetables, sauces and baking. It tenderizes tough cuts of meat and, used in baking, it yields a moist texture and gives a longer shelf life.

BEEF STEW

COMFORT FOOD AT ITS BEST!

¼ cup	flour	60 mL
1 tsp.	salt	5 mL
½ tsp.	pepper	2 mL
1½ lbs.	cubed stewing beef	750 g
¼ cup	vegetable oil	60 mL
2	medium onions, sliced	2
1	garlic clove, minced	1
12 oz.	beer (1 bottle)	340 mL
1 tbsp.	soy sauce	15 mL
1 tbsp.	Worcestershire sauce	15 mL
½ tsp.	thyme	2 mL
2	bay leaves	2
2 cups	tomato juice	500 mL
2 cups	water	500 mL
4	carrots, peeled & sliced	4
½	turnip, peeled & cubed	½
4	parsnips, peeled & sliced	4
3	potatoes, peeled & diced	3
	flour & water for thickening (1 part flour to 2 parts cold water)	

- In a plastic bag, combine flour, salt and pepper. Drop cubed beef into bag and shake to dredge cubes.
- In a large heavy saucepan, heat oil. Add beef cubes and brown. Add onion and garlic; cook until onions are translucent.
- Add beer, soy sauce, Worcestershire sauce, thyme, bay leaves, tomato juice and water. Bring to a boil. Reduce heat; simmer, covered, for 2 hours.
- Add carrots, turnip, parsnips and potatoes. Continue to simmer until all vegetables are tender, about 1 hour. Remove bay leaves.
- Shake flour and water in a covered container. Add to stew and cook until thickened.
- Serve with Parsley Dumplings, page 115.

NOTE   Add vegetables, omit or decrease as desired.

YIELD   **6 SERVING**

PARSLEY DUMPLINGS

LIGHT, FLUFFY AND TENDER

1	egg	1
½ cup	water	125 mL
1 cup	all-purpose flour	250 mL
2 tsp.	baking powder	10 mL
½ tsp.	salt	2 mL
1 tbsp.	finely chopped parsley	15 mL

- In a small bowl, beat egg and water together with a fork
- Combine flour, baking powder, salt and parsley. Add to egg mixture. Combine lightly.
- Drop batter by large spoonfuls on top of hot, cooked stew. Cover and let steam for 10 minutes. Serve hot with stew.

YIELD   **8 LARGE DUMPLINGS**

SWEET 'N' SOUR STEW

TANGY AND SWEET – SATISFYING AND FLAVORFUL

2 tbsp.	flour	30 mL
½ tsp.	salt	2 mL
1½ lbs.	round steak, cubed	675 g
2 tbsp.	vegetable oil	30 mL
1½ cups	beef stock	375 mL
5½ oz.	can tomato paste	156 mL
2 tbsp.	brown sugar	30 mL
¼ cup	vinegar	60 mL
1 tbsp.	Worcestershire sauce	15 mL
1	onion, chopped	1
3	carrots, chopped	3
2 cups	EACH potatoes & turnips, diced	500 mL
¼ tsp.	black pepper	1 mL

- In a plastic bag, combine flour and salt. Add beef and shake to coat.
- In a Dutch oven, heat oil and brown meat. Reduce heat to low.
- Add stock, tomato paste, sugar, vinegar, Worcestershire sauce and onion. Simmer for 45 minutes. Add remaining ingredients. Cook for 45 minutes, or until tender.

YIELD   **6 SERVINGS**

IRISH LAMB STEW

TENDER LAMB IN A RICH BROTH – A CLASSIC WITH DUMPLINGS

1 tbsp.	vegetable oil	15 mL
1½ lbs.	lamb, cut into 1" (2.5 cm) cubes	750 g
2	onions, chopped	2
4	potatoes, peeled, cubed	4
4 cups	beef stock	1 L
½ tsp.	salt	2 mL
¼ tsp.	EACH pepper, celery seed, dried marjoram, dried thyme	1 mL
¼ cup	flour	60 mL
½ cup	cold water	125 mL
10 oz.	package frozen peas	285 g

- In a Dutch oven, heat oil and brown meat. Add onions, potatoes, stock, spices and herbs. Cook on low for 1 hour, or until vegetables are tender.
- Shake flour with water until smooth. Stir into stew with the peas.
- Increase heat; stir and cook until gravy is thickened.
- Add dumplings if desired, see recipe below.

YIELD   4 – 6 SERVINGS

BUTTERMILK DUMPLINGS

FOR HERBED DUMPLINGS, ADD CHOPPED PARSLEY, THYME OR CHIVES

1 cup	all-purpose flour	250 mL
1½ tsp.	baking powder	7 mL
½ tsp.	salt	2 mL
½ cup	buttermilk	125 mL

- In a medium bowl, combine flour, baking powder and salt.
- Gradually stir in buttermilk until a light, soft dough is formed.
- Carefully drop small spoonfuls of dough into cooked stew. Cover and simmer for an additional 15 minutes.

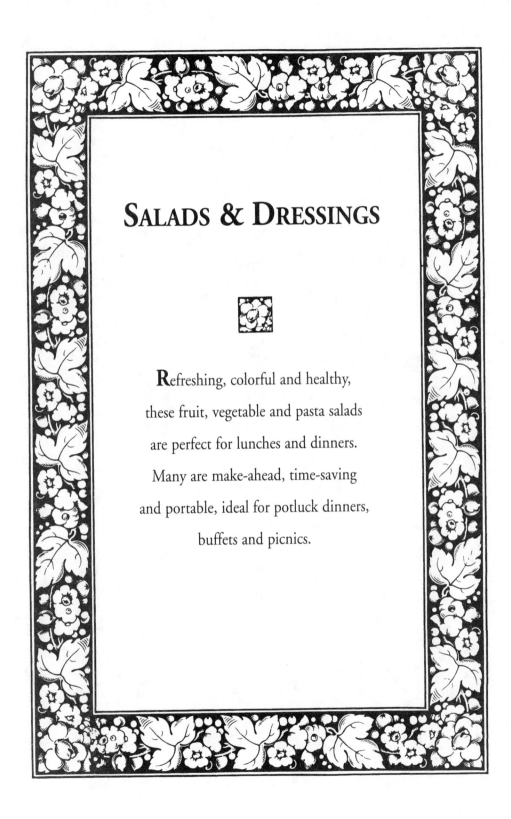

Salads & Dressings

Refreshing, colorful and healthy,
these fruit, vegetable and pasta salads
are perfect for lunches and dinners.
Many are make-ahead, time-saving
and portable, ideal for potluck dinners,
buffets and picnics.

TOMATO ASPIC

SPICY AND COLORFUL – A BUFFET FAVORITE!

5 tsp.	unflavored gelatin	25 mL
¼ cup	cold water	60 mL
2 cups	tomato juice	500 mL
1 tsp.	sugar	5 mL
2 tbsp.	lemon juice	30 mL
¼ tsp.	garlic powder	1 mL
¼ tsp.	paprika	1 mL
¼ tsp.	cayenne pepper	1 mL
¼ tsp.	celery salt	1 mL
¾ cup	grated carrots	175 mL
¼ cup	chopped kalamata olives (optional)	60 mL
½ cup	chopped celery	125 mL
2	green onions, chopped	2

- Soak gelatin in cold water.
- In a saucepan, combine tomato juice, sugar, lemon juice and spices. Bring to a boil. Remove from heat.
- Add gelatin mixture. Blend well.
- Chill. When juice begins to thicken add vegetables.
- Pour into a shallow 6-cup (1.5 L) jelly mold. Chill.
- To serve, unmold and garnish.

VARIATIONS Replace kalamata olives with chopped green olives if you prefer.

Replace carrots with diced avocado or diced red or yellow peppers. Add ½ cup (125 mL) small shrimp or flaked crab.

YIELD **6 SERVINGS**

CREAMY CUCUMBER JELLIED SALAD

LIGHT AND REFRESHING FOR A SUMMER DAY

6 oz.	pkg. lemon gelatin	170 g
1 cup	boiling water	250 mL
1 tbsp.	vinegar	15 mL
1	medium cucumber, chopped	1
1	medium onion, chopped	1
1 cup	small-curd cottage cheese	250 mL
1 cup	mayonnaise-type salad dressing	250 mL
½ cup	chopped walnuts	125 mL

- Dissolve gelatin in boiling water. Add vinegar. Stir until well mixed.
- Chill until partially set. Add remaining ingredients. Mix well.
- Pour into a 6-cup (1.5 L) serving dish or mold. Chill until firm.

YIELD   *6 – 8 SERVINGS*

ZESTY CUCUMBER LIME JELLIED SALAD

COLORFUL, REFRESHING AND TASTY

6 oz.	pkg. lime gelatin	170 g
2 cups	boiling water	500 mL
1 tbsp.	vinegar OR lemon juice	15 mL
1 cup	mayonnaise	250 mL
1 cup	coarsely grated cucumber	250 mL
1 tbsp.	grated onion	15 mL
1 tbsp.	prepared horseradish	15 mL

- Dissolve gelatin in boiling water. Add vinegar and mayonnaise. Chill until partially set.
- Whip gelatin until fluffy. Add cucumber, onion and horseradish.
- Pour into a 4-cup (1 L) mold. Chill until set.

YIELD   *6 – 8 SERVINGS*

BEET HORSERADISH JELLIED SALAD

DELICIOUS SERVED AT A SUMMER PICNIC OR WITH ROAST BEEF!

14 oz.	can diced beets	398 mL
1 tbsp.	unflavored gelatin (1 env.)	7 g
¼ cup	cold water	60 mL
½ tsp.	salt	2 mL
¼ cup	sugar	60 mL
¼ cup	vinegar	60 mL
¾ cup	finely chopped celery	175 mL
1 tbsp.	minced onion	15 mL
1 tbsp.	horseradish	15 mL

- Drain beets. Reserve liquid. Measure reserved liquid and if necessary add water to measure ¾ cup (175 mL).
- In a saucepan, sprinkle gelatin over the ¼ cup (60 mL) cold water. Stir over low heat until gelatin dissolves. Remove from heat. Add salt, sugar and vinegar. Combine well.
- Add beet liquid to gelatin mixture; stir to combine well. Chill until mixture just begins to set.
- Gently stir in celery, onion and horseradish.
- Pour into a lightly greased 3-cup (750 mL) jelly mold. Chill until set.
- To serve, unmold and garnish as desired.

YIELD   16 SERVINGS

Spicy and pungent, horseradish has been used for over 3,000 years – as a condiment, an aphrodisiac, a bitter herb for Passover, a remedy for rheumatism, backaches and headaches. Horseradish is a traditional accompaniment to roast beef, oysters and some fish. It is available preserved in vinegar (white) or in beet juice (red). Buy fresh horseradish roots that are firm and free of blemishes. Refrigerate in plastic and peel before using.

CREAMY HORSERADISH MOLDED SALAD

DELICIOUS WITH ROAST BEEF OR BARBECUED STEAK

3 oz.	pkg. lemon gelatin	85 g
1 cup	boiling water	250 mL
1 tsp.	salt	5 mL
2 tbsp.	vinegar	30 mL
1 cup	prepared horseradish	250 mL
1 cup	whipping cream, whipped	250 mL

- Dissolve gelatin in boiling water. Add salt, vinegar and horseradish. Chill until partially set.
- Fold in whipped cream. Pour into a 6-cup (1.5 L) mold. Chill until set.

YIELD   *6 – 8 SERVINGS*

SPICED CRANBERRY MOLD

SUPERB WITH TURKEY OR ROAST PORK – BEAUTIFUL COLOR

3 oz.	pkg. cranberry gelatin	85 g
1 cup	boiling water	250 mL
½ cup	cold water	125 mL
¼ cup	blanched, slivered almonds	60 mL
1	apple, peeled, diced	1
½ stalk	celery, chopped	½ stalk
¼ cup	whole-berry cranberry sauce	60 mL
¼ tsp.	ground cinnamon	1 mL
⅛ tsp.	ground cloves	0.5 mL

- Dissolve gelatin in boiling water. Stir in cold water. Chill until partially set.
- Combine remaining ingredients. Add to partially set gelatin. Pour into a 4-cup (1 L) mold. Chill until set.
- When set, unmold and garnish.

YIELD   *6 – 8 SERVINGS*

RHUBARB STRAWBERRY MOLD

VIVID ROSY COLOR AND GORGEOUS PRESENTATION

4 cups	chopped rhubarb	1 L
1 cup	water	250 mL
½ cup	sugar	125 mL
6 oz.	pkg. strawberry gelatin	170 g
1	orange, zest of	1
½ cup	orange juice	125 mL
1 cup	sliced fresh strawberries	250 mL
	lettuce leaves for garnish	
	strawberries for garnish	
	French vanilla OR strawberry yogurt	

- In a medium saucepan, over medium heat, cook and stir rhubarb, water and sugar until rhubarb is tender. Remove from heat.
- Stir in gelatin until dissolved. Add orange zest and juice. Chill until partially set. Stir in strawberries.
- Pour into a well-oiled 6-cup (1.5 L) ring mold. Refrigerate until set.
- Unmold onto a lettuce-lined tray and garnish with strawberries. Place yogurt in a small bowl that will fit in the center of the mold.

YIELD   *8 – 10 SERVINGS*

Commercial gelatin became widely available in the early 20th century. In the 1930s, flavored gelatin powders appeared, causing a great increase in the variety and availability of molded gelatin salads and desserts. Ginger ale was often added to created sparkling salads. When using fruit in gelatin preparations, it is important to know that raw papaya, kiwi and pineapple contain an enzyme that keeps the gelatin from setting. However, canned, or thoroughly cooked, these fruits may be used in gelatin salads and desserts.

COTTAGE CHEESE JELLIED SALAD

A SUMMER FAVORITE!

3 oz.	pkg. orange OR lemon gelatin	85 g
1 cup	boiling water	250 mL
½ cup	mayonnaise	125 mL
1 cup	cottage cheese	250 mL
1 cup	drained crushed pineapple	250 mL
½ cup	chopped walnuts	125 mL

- Dissolve gelatin in boiling water. Add mayonnaise; whisk to blend; chill until mixture just begins to set.
- Add cottage cheese, pineapple and walnuts. Combine well.
- Pour gelatin mixture into a lightly oiled 4-cup (1 L) jelly mold or a clear glass bowl. Chill.

YIELD   **6 SERVINGS**

JELLIED RICE SALAD

JELLIED FRUIT SALADS HAVE BEEN POPULAR FOR GENERATIONS
— RICE ADDS AN INTERESTING VARIATION

3 oz.	pkg. gelatin (any flavor)	85 g
1 cup	boiling water	250 mL
14 oz.	can pineapple tidbits, juice reserved	398 mL
1 cup	cooked rice	250 mL
8 oz.	pkg. miniature marshmallows	250 g
1 tsp.	lemon juice	5 mL
1	apple, chopped	1
1 cup	whipping cream, whipped	250 mL

- In a mixing bowl, dissolve gelatin in boiling water. Add pineapple juice and enough water to make 1 cup (250 mL). Chill until partially set.
- Combine rice, marshmallows, lemon juice, apple and pineapple.
- Fold rice mixture into gelatin. Fold in whipped cream. Chill.

YIELD   **6 – 8 SERVINGS**

24-HOUR FRUIT SALAD

A PREPARE-AHEAD PLEASER THAT MAY BE SERVED WITH A MAIN COURSE OR
AS A DESSERT – CHILDREN LOVE THIS LIGHT, FLUFFY CONFECTION

1	egg	1
2 tbsp.	sugar	30 mL
2 tbsp.	lemon juice	30 mL
1/8 tsp.	salt	0.5 mL
1/2 cup	whipping cream, whipped	125 mL
48	miniature marshmallows	48
14 oz.	can pineapple tidbits, drained	398 mL
1 cup	seedless raisins	250 mL
8	maraschino cherries, halved (optional)	8
1/2 cup	slivered almonds	125 mL

- In a double boiler, beat the egg. Stir in sugar, lemon juice and salt. Cook over boiling water for 5 minutes, stirring frequently. Cool.
- Fold cooled lemon mixture into whipped cream. Fold in the marshmallows and fruit.
- Refrigerate overnight.
- To serve, fold in almonds.

VARIATIONS For larger groups, double the amounts. Various fruits may be included, but bananas should be added just prior to serving.

YIELD *12 SERVINGS*

A symbol of hospitality for centuries, pineapples originated in South and Central America. Juicy and flavorful, they also aid digestion and are a natural anti-inflammatory. An excellent source of manganese and a good source of B vitamins, thiamin and riboflavin, pineapples also contain vitamins A and C. Pineapples are picked ripe. The flesh closer to the base has a higher sugar content and is more tender and sweeter. Choose pineapples that feel slightly soft, with crisp green leaves. Only canned pineapple can be used in gelatin mixtures – a natural enzyme in fresh and frozen pineapple prevents gelatin from setting.

Ambrosia Salad

LIGHT AND COLORFUL – AN OLD FAMILY FAVORITE AS A SALAD OR DESSERT

1 cup	sour cream	250 mL
10 oz.	can mandarin oranges, drained	284 mL
1 cup	pineapple tidbits, drained	250 mL
1 cup	miniature marshmallows	250 mL
1 cup	flaked coconut	250 mL
1 cup	green seedless grapes, halved	250 mL

- In a medium bowl, combine all ingredients.
- Refrigerate for 6 hours or overnight before serving.

YIELD   6 SERVINGS

Fresh Fruit Nestled in Barley

BARLEY ADDS NUTTY FLAVOR AND CHEWY TEXTURE TO THIS FRUIT SALAD

2 cups	cooked pearl barley	500 mL
1	apple, cored, diced	1
1	orange, peeled, chopped	1
1 cup	halved strawberries	250 mL
1 cup	seedless grapes	250 mL
1 cup	crushed pineapple	250 mL
2 tbsp.	brown sugar	30 mL
1 tbsp.	lemon juice	15 mL
	yogurt & mint leaves for garnish	

- In a large bowl, gently toss barley with fruit.
- Combine sugar and lemon juice. Gently stir into fruit. Chill for 4 hours.
- To serve, garnish with a dollop of yogurt and a sprig of mint leaves.

YIELD   5 – 6 SERVINGS

WHEAT SALAD

GREAT AS A SALAD OR DESSERT

2 cups	dried wheat berries	500 mL
8 oz.	cream cheese	250 g
14 oz.	can crushed pineapple	398 mL
2 x 4 oz.	pkgs. vanilla instant pudding	2 x 113 g
3 tbsp.	lemon juice	45 mL
1½ cups	chopped walnuts (optional)	375 mL
4 cups	whipped cream OR whipped topping	1 L

- Place wheat in a saucepan. Cover with water. Soak overnight.
- The next day, bring wheat and water to a gentle boil. Cook slowly for 2 hours, or until wheat is tender. Drain and cool.
- In a mixing bowl, combine cheese, pineapple, puddings, lemon juice and walnuts. Mix well.
- Add cooked wheat. Fold in whipped cream. Chill.

NOTE   This recipe is easily halved with favorable results. Any leftovers refrigerate well for 2-3 days.

VARIATIONS   2 cups (500 mL) of mashed cottage cheese can be substituted for the cream cheese. For an interesting variation, substitute pistachio instant pudding for the vanilla instant pudding.

YIELD   **8 – 10 SERVINGS**

Wheat berries are whole wheat kernels with the bran and germ intact. Very nutritious, they may be cooked and used instead of rice in pilafs or as a cereal or to add crunchy texture to breads and stuffings. Most commercially available wheat berries are hard red winter wheat. Spelt and kamut wheat berries, ancient grains, are also available. For very firm wheat berries, for use in some salads, do not presoak and cook for only 1 hour.

Apple, Raisin & Date Salad

Honey, cinnamon and banana create a lovely mellow dressing

Yogurt Banana Dressing:

½ cup	plain yogurt	125 mL
1	small banana, mashed	1
1 tbsp.	lemon juice	15 mL
1 tbsp.	liquid honey	15 mL
½ tsp.	ground cinnamon	2 mL
2	apples, peeled, cored, diced	2
¼ cup	raw sunflower seeds	60 mL
¼ cup	unsweetened flaked coconut	60 mL
½ cup	golden raisins	125 mL
½ cup	finely chopped dates	125 mL

- **For dressing**, blend all ingredients together.
- In a small bowl, combine salad ingredients. Pour dressing over; mix well.

VARIATIONS   ***Carrot Apple Salad*** – Substitute 2 cups (500 mL) grated carrots for 1 apple; substitute ¼ tsp. (1 mL) prepared mustard for the cinnamon.

YIELD   ***6 SERVINGS***

 For over 5,000 years dates have been an important part of Middle Eastern and African cuisine. They also grow now in California and Arizona. Buy whole, unpitted, fresh or dried dates for the best quality. They should be plump and shiny, with no sugar crystals or mold on the surface. Sliced or chopped dates add sweetness and rich, deep flavor to meat and vegetable dishes, as well as to cereals, sandwiches and desserts. High in sugar and a good source of protein and iron, dates also make very good snacks for campers and hikers.

FRUIT SALAD

ANISE ADDS A DISTINCTIVE, SWEET LICORICE FLAVOR
TO YOUR FAVORITE SEASONAL FRUITS

2 cups	water	500 mL
1 cup	sugar	250 mL
¼ cup	lemon juice	60 mL
½ tsp.	salt	2 mL
2 tbsp.	ground anise	30 mL
14 oz.	can pineapple tidbits	398 mL
1 cup	of each type of chopped fruit*	250 mL

- In a saucepan, combine water, sugar, lemon juice, salt and anise. Simmer for 20 minutes. Cool.
- Combine undrained pineapple with fruit. Add sauce and mix gently. Chill until ready to serve. This salad keeps well, refrigerated, in an airtight container.

NOTE * *Suggested fruits*: watermelon, cantaloupe, honeydew, grapes, blueberries, apples and oranges. Fruits that tend to soften, like bananas, kiwi and strawberries, should be added just prior to serving.

YIELD *6 – 8 SERVINGS*

FRUIT IN RUM SAUCE

A LIGHT, FRESH SUMMER SALAD WITH A TANGY, LEMONY SAUCE

1	cantaloupe	1
1	honeydew melon	1
½	watermelon	½
1 cup	sugar	250 mL
½ cup	water	125 mL
1 tbsp.	grated lemon zest	15 mL
½ cup	lemon juice	125 mL
½ cup	light rum	125 mL
2 cups	blueberries	500 mL

FRUIT IN RUM SAUCE
(CONTINUED)

- Peel and seed melons. Cut fruit into balls or chop.
- In a saucepan, combine sugar and water. Bring to a boil; reduce heat; simmer for 5 minutes. Add lemon zest; cool. Add lemon juice and rum.
- Combine melon balls with blueberries. Pour cooled liquid over fruit. Chill several hours. Serve.

YIELD   **12 – 16 SERVINGS**

WATERMELON SUMMER SALAD

A VERY REFRESHING MEDITERRANEAN SALAD WITH A BEAUTIFUL PRESENTATION

1	red onion, sliced in thin vertical slivers	1
3-4	limes, juice of	3-4
1 bunch	fresh cilantro, coarsely chopped	1 bunch
8 oz.	feta, cubed, or more to taste	250 g
½-1 cup	kalamata olives	125-250 mL
4 lb.	watermelon, rind removed, cut into bite-sized pieces (4 cups/1 L)	2 kg
	salt & pepper to taste	

- Place onion in a small bowl; stir in lime juice and half of the cilantro. Marinate in refrigerator for at least 1 hour.
- Place feta cheese, olives and remainder of cilantro in a large bowl.
- Add onion mixture, watermelon, salt and pepper. (A pinch of salt helps watermelon retain water, which the lime juice tends to draw out.)

VARIATIONS   For a more traditional version, add ¼ cup (60 mL) olive oil with the feta.

Substitute flat-leaf parsley, mint, rosemary OR basil, OR half parsley and half mint, for cilantro.

Substitute juice of 2 lemons for lime juice OR use 2-3 tbsp. (30-45 mL) red wine or balsamic vinegar, or more to taste.

For a sweeter salad, use havarti cheese and halved green grapes. Omit olives.

YIELD   **8 – 10 SERVINGS**

SENSATIONAL STRAWBERRY SALAD

SO BEAUTIFUL AND SO GOOD – IT'S ADDICTIVE

2 cups	strawberries, thickly sliced, quartered or halved	500 mL
1 cup	blueberries (optional)	250 mL
1 cup	orange segments, membranes removed (optional)	250 mL
8 cups	washed, torn fresh spinach	2 L

ZESTY WORCESTERSHIRE DRESSING:

⅓ cup	sugar	75 mL
2 tbsp.	EACH sesame & poppy seeds	30 mL
3 tbsp.	minced onion	45 mL
¼ cup	Worcestershire sauce	60 mL
¼ tsp.	paprika	1 mL
½ cup	vegetable oil	125 mL
¼ cup	cider vinegar	60 mL

- In a large bowl, gently toss strawberries, blueberries and orange segments with spinach.
- **For dressing**, combine all ingredients in a small jar; cover and shake well.
- When ready to serve, pour dressing over salad and toss gently.

VARIATIONS   Substitute crisp Romaine or mixed greens for the spinach. Add toasted pecans.

For ***Strawberry & Feta Salad***, add 1 cup (250 mL) crumbled feta cheese.

For ***Strawberry Stilton Salad***, add ¾ cup (175 mL) crumbled Stilton, or use Roquefort, Gorgonzola or blue cheese.

YIELD   ***8 – 10 SERVINGS***

See photograph on page 17.

SPRINGTIME SALAD

COLORFUL, REFRESHING, TASTY

4 cups	torn lettuce leaves	1 L
2 cups	chopped broccoli florets	500 mL
1 cup	sliced strawberries	250 mL
2	navel oranges, membranes & pith removed, segmented	2

HONEY POPPY SEED DRESSING:

2 tbsp.	liquid honey	30 mL
2 tbsp.	vinegar	30 mL
2 tsp.	poppy seeds	10 mL
2 tbsp.	fresh lemon juice	30 mL
1½ tsp.	Dijon mustard	7 mL
2 tsp.	minced onion	10 mL
pinch	salt	pinch
⅓ cup	vegetable oil	75 mL

- Place salad ingredients in a bowl.
- **For dressing**, place all ingredients in a blender. Process thoroughly.
- To serve, toss dressing over salad ingredients to coat lightly.
- Refrigerate any additional dressing.

VARIATION   Add 1 cup (250 mL) of blueberries to the salad.

YIELD   *4 – 7 SERVINGS*

See photograph on page 175.

SALAD OF THE GODS

EXTRA SPECIAL – JUST LIKE ITS NAME

TARRAGON LEMON DRESSING:

½ cup	white wine vinegar	125 mL
¼ cup	vegetable oil	60 mL
1 tbsp.	lemon juice	15 mL
½ tsp.	ground tarragon	2 mL
¼ tsp.	ground marjoram	1 mL
¼ tsp.	salt	1 mL
¼ tsp.	sugar	1 mL
¼ tsp.	pepper	1 mL
1	head romaine lettuce	1
19 oz.	can pineapple chunks	540 mL
20 oz.	can lychees in syrup (optional)	565 g
1	red apple	1
1	orange, peeled & sliced	1
½ lb.	seedless red OR green grapes	250 g

- **For dressing**, at least a day in advance, place all ingredients in a blender. Blend, place in a jar and refrigerate until ready to use.
- Next day, wash lettuce and tear into bite-sized pieces.
- Drain pineapple, reserving liquid. Drain lychees thoroughly.
- Core apple and chop coarsely. Immerse in reserved pineapple juice to prevent discoloring. Prepare orange. Halve grapes.
- Combine pineapple chunks, lychees, drained apple pieces, orange slices and grapes. Toss lightly with some of the dressing.
- Combine the fruit with the lettuce. Toss lightly. Serve with additional dressing on the side.

YIELD   6 SERVINGS

POMEGRANATE & ONION
WITH MIXED GREENS

AN INTERESTING, REFRESHING SALAD FOR POMEGRANATE SEASON

1	pomegranate	1
6 cups	mixed greens	1.5 L
½	sweet onion, thinly sliced	½
¼ cup	toasted pecans OR hazelnuts	60 mL

BALSAMIC RASPBERRY VINAIGRETTE:

1	garlic clove, minced	1
1 tsp.	honey mustard	5 mL
2 tbsp.	raspberry vinegar	30 mL
1 tbsp.	balsamic vinegar	15 mL
1 tbsp.	brown sugar	15 mL
¼ cup	olive oil	60 mL

- Cut pomegranate; separate seeds from the bitter cream-colored membranes.
- In a medium bowl, combine greens, onion and pomegranate seeds.
- **For dressing**, place all ingredients in a blender. Process thoroughly.
- To serve, lightly toss salad with enough dressing to just coat greens. Refrigerate any remaining dressing. Garnish with pecans.

VARIATION   ***Poached Pear & Gorgonzola with Mixed Greens*** – use only ¼ cup (60 mL) minced onion; replace the pomegranate with 2 thinly sliced poached pears. Add ½ cup (125 mL) crumbled Gorgonzola OR blue cheese.

YIELD   *4 SERVINGS*

 To **poach pears**, heat 1 quart (1 L) of water in a medium saucepan; stir in 1 cup (250 mL) sugar until dissolved. Add peeled sliced pears and simmer, uncovered, until tender, about 3-5 minutes. Drain pears and refrigerate until using. Poaching liquid may be flavored with vanilla, lemon zest, cinnamon or balsamic vinegar.

ORANGE-ALMOND LETTUCE SALAD

SUGARED ALMONDS AND ORANGES ACCENT FRESH VEGETABLES

¼ cup	sliced blanched almonds	60 mL
2 tsp.	sugar	10 mL
1 head	lettuce, torn into bite-sized pieces	1 head
3	radishes, sliced	3
3	green onions, chopped	3
2 stalks	celery, chopped	2 stalks
¼	English cucumber, sliced	¼
1 cup	orange segments, membranes & pith removed OR 10 oz. (284 mL) can mandarin orange segments, drained, juice reserved	250 mL

GARLIC ORANGE DRESSING:

¼ cup	extra-virgin olive oil	60 mL
2 tbsp.	reserved orange juice	30 mL
1 tbsp.	sugar	15 mL
3 tbsp.	vinegar	45 mL
2	garlic cloves, minced	2
½ tsp.	salt	2 mL
¼ tsp.	pepper	1 mL

- In a small skillet, over low-medium heat, toast almonds in sugar until sugar melts and almonds are lightly browned. Cool. Set aside.
- In a large bowl, combine lettuce, other vegetables and orange segments.
- **For dressing**, place all ingredients in a blender. Process thoroughly. Pour dressing over vegetables; toss lightly.
- Serve salad sprinkled with toasted almonds.

YIELD   6 – 8 SERVINGS

Spinach Fruit Salad

Light and lovely for sultry summer days

8 oz.	fresh spinach	250 g
⅓ cup	mayonnaise	75 mL
1 tbsp.	lemon juice	15 mL
¼ tsp.	ground ginger	1 mL
3	pears, cubed	3
1 cup	orange segments, membranes & pith removed, OR 10 oz. (284 mL) can mandarin oranges, drained	250 mL
⅓ cup	seedless raisins	75 mL
⅓ cup	sunflower seeds	75 mL

- Wash and tear spinach into bite-sized pieces.
- In a bowl, combine mayonnaise, lemon juice and ginger.
- Add remaining ingredients to mayonnaise. Toss and serve over spinach.

VARIATION Substitute dried cranberries for the raisins. Substitute slivered almonds for the sunflower seeds.

YIELD *4 – 6 SERVINGS*

 Spinach was brought to North America from Spain. In Italy, spinach is so popular that recipes featuring it are often called "à la Florentine". Rich in iron, vitamins A and C, its slightly bitter flavor is enhanced by both tart and rich flavors – cheeses, butter, lemon, garlic, eggs, oysters, mushrooms and bacon. Spinach stars in soups, salads, pasta and seafood dishes.

Spinach Apple Salad with Chutney Dressing

The zesty dressing brings out the best in these ingredients

4 cups	fresh spinach, washed, dried	1 L
1	Granny Smith apple, diced	1
2	green onions, chopped	2
	unsalted dry roasted peanuts OR raw sunflower seeds	

Chutney Dressing:

2 tbsp.	lemon juice	30 mL
1 tbsp.	red wine vinegar	15 mL
2 tbsp.	peach OR mango chutney	30 mL
½ tsp.	curry powder	2 mL
pinch	cayenne	pinch
⅛ tsp.	turmeric	0.5 mL
¼ tsp.	sugar	1 mL
¼ cup	olive oil	60 mL

- Place spinach in a salad bowl. Add apple and onions.
- **For dressing**, place all ingredients, except oil, in a blender. Process thoroughly. While continuing to process, slowly add oil.
- To serve, toss salad with dressing, coating lightly. Sprinkle with peanuts. Refrigerate any extra dressing.

YIELD   4 SERVINGS

See photograph on page 105.

SPINACH WALDORF SALAD

TRY VARIOUS FRUITS TO FIT THE SEASON

POPPY SEED DRESSING:

½ cup	sugar	125 mL
1 tsp.	dry mustard	5 mL
1 tsp.	salt	5 mL
⅓ cup	vinegar	75 mL
½	medium onion, finely chopped	½
1 cup	vegetable oil	250 mL
2 tbsp.	poppy seeds	30 mL
6 cups	fresh spinach, rinsed	1.5 L
2 tbsp.	lemon juice	30 mL
1	red apple	1
1	yellow OR green apple	1
2 stalks	celery, chopped	2 stalks
¼ cup	raisins	60 mL
½ cup	grapes	125 mL
¼ cup	pecan pieces (optional)	60 mL

- **For dressing**, in a blender, combine sugar, mustard, salt, vinegar and onion. Add oil slowly while blending. Add poppy seeds and continue to beat until thick and well blended.
- Tear spinach into bite-sized pieces and place in a salad bowl.
- Pour lemon juice into a small bowl. Core and cube apples and place in lemon juice. Stir to coat apple pieces to prevent discoloring. Drain off extra juice. Add celery, raisins and grapes to apples. Add enough dressing to thoroughly coat fruit.
- When ready to serve, toss fruit with spinach. Add pecans if desired. Serve with additional dressing on the side.

YIELD   6 SERVINGS

WALDORF SALAD

A FAVORITE FOR A LADIES' LUNCHEON

2 cups	diced apple	500 mL
1 cup	diced celery	250 mL
½ cup	chopped walnuts	125 mL
½ cup	raisins OR halved, seedless grapes	125 mL
½ cup	mayonnaise	125 mL
2 tsp.	lemon juice	10 mL
6-8	lettuce leaves	6-8

- In a salad bowl, combine apple, celery, walnuts and raisins.
- **For dressing**, mix mayonnaise with lemon juice.
- Pour dressing over apple mixture. Mix gently.
- On serving plates, arrange lettuce leaves into cups. Fill cups with salad.

YIELD   *6 – 8 SERVINGS*

ORANGE ONION SALAD

SWEET AND SHARP – A DELICIOUS COMBINATION

2-3	oranges, peeled, quartered, sliced	2-3
½	sweet onion, finely chopped	½
½ cup	mayonnaise	125 mL
2 tbsp.	vinegar	30 mL
⅓ cup	sugar	75 mL
¼ cup	milk	60 mL
2 tbsp.	poppy seeds	30 mL
	mixed greens OR spinach leaves	

- In a salad bowl, combine oranges and onion.
- **For dressing**, combine remaining ingredients, except lettuce.
- Combine part of the dressing with the oranges and onion.
- Serve on a bed of mixed greens. Refrigerate any remaining dressing.

YIELD   *6 SERVINGS*

See photograph opposite.

Orange Onion Salad, page 138
French Onion Soup, page 40

Jicama Orange Salad

CRISP JICAMA HAS AN AFFINITY WITH ONIONS AND ORANGES

1	jicama, peeled, julienned	1
½	cucumber, peeled, halved lengthwise, thinly sliced	½
1	small red onion, thinly sliced	1
3	oranges, peeled, quartered, sliced	3
½ head	lettuce, in bite-sized pieces	½ head
¼ cup	vegetable oil	60 mL
3 tbsp.	rice vinegar	45 mL
½ tsp.	salt	2 mL
¼ tsp.	freshly ground pepper	1 mL

- In a large salad bowl, combine the first 5 ingredients.
- **For dressing**, in a small jar, combine remaining ingredients.
- When ready to serve, toss salad with dressing.

YIELD   *6 SERVINGS*

Jicama, from Central and South America, looks like a flattened brown turnip. It has the crisp texture of a water chestnut, with a mild sweet, nutty flavor. It may be eaten raw or quickly sautéed, steamed, baked or boiled. To prepare, scrub, then peel and also remove the thin layer under the skin. Cut into slices, matchsticks or cubes. Citrus juices and hot pepper sauces complement the mild flavor of jicama.

CARROT FRUIT SALAD

A GOOD CHOICE FOR A WINTERTIME SIDE DISH

1	large navel orange, peeled, segmented, membranes & pith removed	1
1	medium carrot, coarsely grated	1
1	Red Delicious apple, cored, chopped	1
½ stalk	celery, chopped	½ stalk
¼ cup	seedless raisins	60 mL
2 tbsp.	mayonnaise	30 mL
2 tsp.	lemon juice	10 mL
	leaf lettuce	

- Cut orange segments into 4 pieces.
- In a salad bowl, combine oranges, carrot, apple, celery and raisins.
- **For dressing**, in a small bowl combine mayonnaise and lemon juice.
- Pour dressing over fruit; toss lightly. Chill until ready to serve.
- To serve, spoon salad onto a lettuce-lined platter.

YIELD   *4 SERVINGS*

CARROT ORANGE SALAD

THIS WORKS — INTENSE COLOR AND GREAT FLAVOR

4 cups	grated carrots, about 8 carrots	1 L
1 cup	raisins OR chopped dates	250 mL
2-3	oranges, peeled, quartered, sliced	2-3
½ cup	mayonnaise	125 mL
3 tbsp.	orange juice	45 mL
2 tbsp.	lemon juice	30 mL
1 tbsp.	honey	15 mL
½ tsp.	salt	2 mL
¼-½ tsp.	cinnamon (optional)	1-2 mL

Carrot Orange Salad

(Continued)

- In a salad bowl, combine grated carrots, raisins and orange slices.
- **For dressing**, combine remaining ingredients.
- Pour dressing over salad. Chill at least 1 hour before serving.

VARIATIONS Add ½ cup (125 mL) of grated red onion. Try ½ mayonnaise and ½ yogurt for a lighter dressing.

YIELD ***6 – 8 SERVINGS***

Roasted Beet & Orange Salad

A COLORFUL, REFRESHING SALAD GREAT FOR WINTERTIME!

4	medium beets, oven roasted & peeled	4
2	navel oranges, peeled, segmented, membranes & pith removed	2
1	sweet onion, sliced	1
	salt & pepper to taste	

RED WINE GARLIC DRESSING:

¼ cup	red wine vinegar	60 mL
3 tbsp.	extra-virgin olive oil	45 mL
2	garlic cloves, minced	2
1 tsp.	grated orange zest	5 mL

- Cut beets into small wedges
- Cut orange segments into quarters.
- In a salad bowl, combine beets, oranges and onion.
- **For dressing**, blend all ingredients. Pour enough of the dressing over beet mixture to coat ingredients. Season with salt and pepper.
- Let stand at room temperature for an hour to allow flavors to blend.

NOTE Roasting rather than boiling beets retains better flavor. Trim beets of all but 2" (5 cm) of stalk. Place washed, still-wet beets in a foil-lined baking pan. Drizzle beets with olive oil and sprinkle with salt. Fold foil over beets to seal. Roast at 350°F (180°C) for 1½-2 hours, or until tender.

YIELD ***4 – 6 SERVINGS***

CAULIFLOWER BROCCOLI SALAD

A HEALTHY, COLORFUL, CRISP, TAKE-ALONG SALAD

2 cups	EACH chopped broccoli & cauliflower	500 mL
½	red onion, chopped	½
½ cup	dried cranberries OR 1 cup (250 mL) halved green OR red grapes	125 mL
⅓ cup	sunflower seeds	75 mL
2 tbsp.	toasted flax seeds	30 mL
⅓ cup	mayonnaise	75 mL
1 tbsp.	raspberry vinegar	15 mL
1 tbsp.	sugar	15 mL

- In a salad bowl, combine vegetables, cranberries and seeds.
- **For dressing**, combine remaining ingredients.
- Toss salad with dressing. Chill for several hours before serving.

YIELD   ***6 SERVINGS***

SUNNY BROCCOLI SALAD

SO GOOD IT'S BECOME A CANADIAN CLASSIC

6 cups	broccoli florets	1.5 L
1 cup	raisins OR dried cranberries	250 mL
½	large red onion, chopped	½
10 slices	bacon, cooked crisp, crumbled	10 slices
1 cup	sunflower seeds OR flaked almonds	250 mL
2 tbsp.	sugar	30 mL
½ cup	mayonnaise	125 mL
2 tbsp.	red wine OR cider vinegar	30 mL

- In a salad bowl, combine broccoli, raisins, onion, bacon and seeds.
- **For dressing**, in a small bowl, whisk together remaining ingredients. Toss salad with dressing. Chill for several hours before serving.

VARIATION   Add strips of red pepper.

                     Omit raisins and add 2 cups (500 mL) grated Cheddar cheese.

YIELD   ***8 SERVINGS***

ONION CUCUMBER SALAD

SOUR CREAM AND DILL ARE SUPERB WITH ONIONS AND CUCUMBERS

2	medium cucumbers, peeled, thinly sliced	2
1	large onion, peeled, thinly sliced	1
½ tsp	salt	2 mL
½ cup	sour cream OR plain yogurt	125 mL
1 tsp.	snipped fresh dill	5 mL
1 tbsp.	vinegar	15 mL
1 tbsp.	sugar	15 mL
¼ tsp.	pepper	1 mL
	greens – spinach, lettuce (optional)	

- A few hours before serving, place sliced vegetables in a colander in the sink. Sprinkle with salt. Let drain for at least an hour.
- **For dressing**, combine remaining ingredients, except greens.
- Transfer vegetables to a bowl. Add dressing and chill for at least an hour before serving to allow flavors to blend. Serve on a bed of greens.

YIELD   6 – 8 SERVINGS

MARINATED ONIONS

SERVE THIS POPULAR SIDE DISH AT A PICNIC OR BEEF BARBECUE!

4	large onions	4
1 cup	vinegar	250 mL
½ cup	white sugar	125 mL
¼ cup	mayonnaise	60 mL
1 tsp.	celery seed	5 mL

- Peel and slice onions. Divide into rings. Place in a glass bowl.
- In a saucepan, combine vinegar and sugar. Bring to a boil. Pour over onions. Refrigerate for a minimum of 6 hours. Drain.
- To serve, stir mayonnaise and celery seed into onions.

YIELD   8 – 10 SERVINGS

CARROT COPPER PENNY SALAD

AN EXCELLENT MAKE-AHEAD BUFFET OR POTLUCK DISH!

8	large carrots, peeled & sliced	8
1	onion, sliced & separated into rings	1
1	green pepper, chopped	1
10 oz.	can tomato soup	284 mL
½ cup	vegetable oil	125 mL
½ cup	sugar	125 mL
¾ cup	vinegar	175 mL
1 tsp.	prepared mustard	5 mL
1 tbsp.	Worcestershire sauce	15 mL
½ tsp.	salt	2 mL
1 tsp.	pepper	5 mL
1 tsp.	dill seed	5 mL

- Cook carrots until tender. Drain. Cool. Add onion and pepper.
- **For dressing**, combine remaining ingredients.
- Pour dressing over vegetables; refrigerate for 12 hours before serving.

YIELD   *8 SERVINGS*

MUSHROOMS & PEPPERS

CRUNCHY AND COLORFUL – GREAT FOR A BARBECUE OR PICNIC

2 cups	sliced mushrooms	500 mL
1	EACH red, yellow & green pepper, diced	1
3	green onions, chopped	3
1 tbsp.	chopped fresh parsley	15 mL
¼ cup	Superb French Dressing, see page 177	60 mL
	salt & pepper to taste	

- Place mushrooms, peppers and onions in a salad bowl.
- Combine parsley, dressing, salt and pepper; mix well.
- Gently toss dressing with vegetables. Serve.

YIELD   *6 SERVINGS*

TOMATO MOZZARELLA SALAD

THIS VERY SIMPLE SALAD IS WONDERFUL WITH FRESH GARDEN TOMATOES –
ITALIAN GRANDMOTHERS HAVE BEEN MAKING IT FOR GENERATIONS!

6	ripe tomatoes, thickly sliced	6
1¼ lbs.	mozzarella cheese, thickly sliced	625 g
8-10	fresh basil leaves, coarsely chopped	8-10
	red wine vinegar (optional)	
¼ cup	extra virgin olive oil, OR more, to taste	60 mL
	salt & freshly ground pepper to taste	

- On a large serving plate or in a shallow bowl, alternate tomato and mozzarella slices.
- Sprinkle with basil and drizzle with vinegar and olive oil. Serve at once.

NOTE   Mozzarella should be sliced about half as thick as tomatoes.

VARIATIONS   Substitute fresh bocconcini, a mild unripened Italian cheese, for the mozzarella.

Substitute 2 tbsp. (30 mL) of chopped fresh oregano for the basil or use it in addition to the basil.

Sprinkle 2-3 tbsp. (30-45 mL) of capers over the salad.

You can omit cheese entirely and enjoy the fresh tomatoes with basil, vinegar and oil or add thinly sliced sweet onions instead of the cheese.

Layer thinly sliced prosciutto alternately with tomatoes and mozzarella.

YIELD   **6 – 8 SERVINGS**

See photograph on page 51.

Fresh mozzarella, made from water buffalo or cow's milk, has a soft texture and sweet, light flavor. It is packed in water or whey and is ideal for salads. Bocconcini, one form of fresh mozzarella, is shaped into small balls and may be marinated in olive oil and herbs.

Regular mozzarella has a drier texture and less delicate flavor. Made from cow's milk, it melts very well and is used for pizzas and lasagne.

LAYERED VEGETABLE SALAD

AN ATTRACTIVE SALAD FOR A BARBECUE OR BUFFET LUNCHEON!

3 cups	shredded salad greens	750 mL
3	green onions, chopped	3
2	medium zucchini, sliced	2
2	large carrots, shredded	2
2 cups	sliced mushrooms	500 mL
1 cup	chopped celery	250 mL
2	medium tomatoes, diced	2
	shredded cheese; crisp, crumbled bacon; chopped green onion OR parsley for garnish	

CREAMY DRESSING:

1 cup	creamed cottage cheese	250 mL
½ cup	sour cream	125 mL
½ cup	plain yogurt (optional)	125 mL
¼ cup	mayonnaise	60 mL
½ tsp.	salt	2 mL
1 tsp.	mustard	5 mL
1 tbsp.	lemon juice	15 mL

- In a clear straight-sided large glass bowl, layer vegetables in order given, leave garnish suggestions until serving time.
- **For dressing**, combine all ingredients, mixing well. Spread over vegetables. Cover with clear plastic wrap. Refrigerate for 4 hours or overnight.
- To serve, garnish with shredded cheese, crumbled bacon, chopped green onion or parsley.
- If desired, toss salad lightly before serving.

YIELD   *8 – 10 SERVINGS*

GREEK SALAD

FRESH, COLORFUL, DELECTABLE!

2	large tomatoes, seeded, cut into wedges	2
1	English cucumber, unpeeled, cut into thick slices	1
1	green pepper, in 1" (2.5 cm) chunks	1
1	sweet white onion, sliced	1
2 stalks	celery, cut into ½" (1.3 cm) diagonal chunks	2 stalks
4 oz.	feta cheese, crumbled	115 g
4 oz.	kalamata olives	115 g

GREEK SALAD DRESSING:

½ cup	olive oil	125 mL
2 tbsp.	lemon juice	30 mL
2 tbsp.	red wine vinegar	30 mL
1	garlic clove, minced	1
½ tsp.	dried oregano	2 mL

- Place salad ingredients in a bowl.
- **For dressing**, combine all ingredients in a blender. Blend.
- To serve, toss dressing over vegetables to coat lightly.
- Pass additional dressing with salad.

YIELD   **6 SERVINGS**

Oregano (wild marjoram) means mountain joy in Greek, and it was used to crown Greek and Roman brides and grooms. Part of the mint family, it is related to sweet marjoram and thyme, but the flavor and aroma are stronger. Oregano has been used to treat infections and it is a very potent anti-oxidant, a very good source of vitamin A plus iron, calcium, manganese, magnesium and vitamin B6.

WILTED SPINACH SALAD

WARM BACON AND CIDER VINEGAR DRESSING – THIS IS BURSTING WITH FLAVOR

10 oz.	fresh spinach, washed, dried	283 g
1 tbsp.	bacon drippings	15 mL
1	small onion, chopped	1
2 tsp.	sugar	10 mL
½ tsp.	salt	2 mL
½ tsp.	dry mustard	2 mL
½ cup	cider vinegar	125 mL
	freshly ground pepper	
6 slices	bacon, cooked crisp, drained, crumbled	6 slices
3	hard-boiled eggs, peeled, chopped	3

- Place spinach in a large salad bowl.
- **For dressing**, in a skillet, heat bacon drippings and sauté onion until soft. Add sugar, salt, mustard and vinegar; continue to cook until sugar is dissolved. Pour hot dressing over spinach.
- Grind pepper over spinach and toss. Garnish with crumbled bacon and chopped eggs.

VARIATION   Omit the eggs and garnish with crumbled feta cheese and pitted ripe olives. Try red wine vinegar in place of cider vinegar. Also try crumbled blue cheese and chopped toasted pecans.

YIELD   ***6 SERVINGS***

Made from fermented apple cider, apple cider vinegar has a spicy, fruit flavor that adds zest to salad dressings. The ancient Romans and the Victorians used cider vinegar with lavender, rosemary and rose petals as a skin tonic and hair rinse. Store vinegar in a cool, dark place.

CAESAR SALAD

A CLASSIC SALAD THAT IS STILL A FAVORITE

CAESAR DRESSING:

½ cup	olive oil	125 mL
2 tbsp.	lemon juice	30 mL
1 tsp.	red wine vinegar	5 mL
2	garlic cloves	2
1 tsp.	Dijon mustard	5 mL
½ tsp.	Worcestershire sauce	2 mL
1	egg	1
4	capers (optional)	4
2 tsp.	anchovy paste (optional)	10 mL
¼ tsp.	salt	1 mL
¼ tsp.	freshly ground pepper	1 mL
1	head Romaine lettuce	1
½ cup	grated Parmesan cheese	125 mL
½ cup	crumbled crisp bacon	125 mL
1 cup	croûtons	250 mL

- **For dressing**, combine all ingredients in a blender. Blend. Refrigerate until ready to use.
- Tear lettuce into bite-sized pieces. Sprinkle with half of the Parmesan cheese and toss well. Pour some of the dressing over and again toss well. Top with bacon bits and croûtons.
- Serve salad with remaining dressing and cheese on the side.

VARIATIONS   *Grilled Chicken Caesar* – omit bacon and add grilled chicken strips.
Grilled Salmon Caesar – omit bacon and add grilled salmon strips.
Lobster, Shrimp or Crab Caesar – omit bacon and add steamed lobster, or crab, grilled or sautéed shrimp.

YIELD   *8 SERVINGS*

See photograph on page 157.

LEBANESE BREAD SALAD

AN ADDICTIVE MIDDLE EASTERN TRADITION – TOASTED PITAS
BECOME TASTY CROÛTONS

½	English cucumber, diced	½
1	red pepper, thinly sliced	1
1 cup	thinly sliced green onion	250 mL
½ cup	sliced radishes	125 mL
1½ cups	coarsely chopped fresh parsley	375 mL
¼ cup	coarsely chopped fresh mint	60 mL
2	garlic cloves, crushed	2
½ tsp.	salt	2 mL
¼ cup	fresh lemon juice	60 mL
½ cup	olive oil	125 mL
¼ tsp.	EACH cinnamon & allspice	1 mL
	salt & pepper to taste	
2 cups	torn romaine lettuce (optional)	500 mL
3	tomatoes, diced	3
3-4	small pitas, opened, oven toasted, broken into bite-sized pieces	3-4

- In a salad bowl, combine cucumber, pepper, onion, radish, parsley and mint. Refrigerate until using.
- **For dressing**, in a small bowl, combine garlic, salt, lemon juice, oil and spices.
- To serve, add dressing to salad; mix well. Add romaine, tomatoes and pita; toss and serve.

YIELD   *8 – 10 SERVINGS*

TABBOULEH

THIS MIDDLE EASTERN DISH DESERVES ITS POPULARITY!

⅔ cup	bulgur (crushed wheat)	150 mL
2 cups	chopped fresh parsley	500 mL
2 tbsp.	chopped fresh mint	30 mL
2	green onions, chopped	2
1	yellow pepper, chopped (optional)	1
¼ cup	olive oil	60 mL
2 tbsp.	lemon juice	30 mL
2	garlic cloves, crushed	2
1	large tomato, chopped & seeded	1
	romaine lettuce leaves	

- Place bulgur in a mixing bowl. Cover with hot water. Set aside for 30 minutes. Drain and squeeze dry.
- Combine bulgur with remaining ingredients, except tomatoes and lettuce leaves. Cover. Refrigerate for 2 hours, stirring occasionally.
- Just before serving add tomatoes. Toss well.
- To eat, tear lettuce into bite-sized pieces and use to scoop up tabbouleh.

YIELD   *12 APPETIZER OR 4 MAIN COURSE SERVINGS*

A symbol of hospitality, mint is used in many Mediterranean dishes. Over 30 species of mint are available, including chocolate mint, but peppermint and spearmint are the most popular. Peppermint has the most intense flavor and scent. Add chopped fresh spearmint to cooked vegetables, scrambled eggs or omelets at the end of the cooking process. Garnish fruit or chocolate desserts with mint sprigs and steep fresh mint in boiling water or with green tea for 2-5 minutes for a refreshing tea.

COLESLAW WITH APPLE

NOTHING IS TASTIER THAN FRESH HOME-GROWN CABBAGE COLESLAW!

4 cups	finely shredded cabbage	1 L
½ cup	chopped red onion	125 mL
1 cup	grated carrots	250 mL
½ cup	raisins (optional)	125 mL
1 tbsp.	sugar	15 mL
½ cup	chopped apple	125 mL
2 tbsp.	mayonnaise	30 mL
2 tbsp.	lemon juice	30 mL
	salt & pepper to taste	

- In a large mixing bowl, combine cabbage, onions, carrots and raisins. Sprinkle with sugar. Refrigerate for 1 hour. Add apple.
- **For dressing**, combine remaining ingredients.
- Pour dressing over cabbage mixture and toss lightly.

YIELD   8 – 10 SERVINGS

24-HOUR BARBECUE COLESLAW

A GREAT MAKE-AHEAD SALAD – CAN YOU HAVE A BARBECUE WITHOUT COLESLAW?

1	large head cabbage, shredded	1
1	green pepper, chopped	1
1	onion, sliced into rings	1
½ cup	sugar	125 mL

MUSTARD DRESSING:

1 cup	vinegar	250 mL
¾ cup	vegetable oil	175 mL
1 tbsp.	EACH sugar, celery seed, salt & dry mustard	15 mL
½ tsp.	turmeric (optional)	2 mL

24-HOUR BARBECUE COLESLAW

(CONTINUED)

- Layer cabbage, green pepper and onion rings in a container with a tight-fitting lid. Sprinkle with ½ cup (125 mL) sugar. Do NOT stir.
- **For dressing**, in a small saucepan, bring vinegar, oil, 1 tbsp. (15 mL) sugar, celery seed, salt and dry mustard to the boiling point. Remove from heat; pour over layered vegetables. Do NOT stir.
- Chill, tightly covered, for at least 24 hours. Mix well before serving.
- Refrigerated, this salad will keep well for several days.

VARIATIONS   Add 2 medium carrots finely shredded.

For *Holiday Coleslaw*, use half red cabbage and half green cabbage.

YIELD   *10 – 12 SERVINGS*

JAPANESE NOODLES COLESLAW

AN INTERESTING BLEND OF FLAVORS AND TEXTURES

1	small cabbage, shredded	1
6	green onions, chopped	6
½ cup	slivered almonds	125 mL
½ cup	raw sunflower seeds	125 mL
¼ cup	vegetable oil	60 mL
¼ cup	vinegar	60 mL
3½ oz.	pkg. Ichiban noodles, original flavor mix	100 g

- In a large bowl, combine cabbage and onions.
- In a skillet, brown almonds and sunflower seeds. Set aside.
- In a small bowl, combine vegetable oil, vinegar and seasoning package from noodles. Toss with vegetables. This can be done up to a day in advance of serving.
- Just prior to serving, crush Ichiban noodles. Add noodles, almonds and sunflower seeds to cabbage. Toss to mix. Serve at once.

YIELD   *8 – 10 SERVINGS*

SAUERKRAUT SALAD

PREPARE THIS LONG-TIME FAVORITE AT LEAST 12 HOURS BEFORE SERVING

14 oz.	can sauerkraut	398 mL
3	green onions, chopped	3
1	green pepper, chopped	1
1	carrot, grated	1
½ cup	sugar	125 mL
1 tsp.	celery salt	5 mL

- Rinse and drain sauerkraut thoroughly.
- In a glass bowl, mix sauerkraut with vegetables. Sprinkle with sugar and celery salt; cover and refrigerate.
- Mix thoroughly before serving.

YIELD   **6 – 8 SERVINGS**

CHICKPEA RED PEPPER SALAD

HIGH FIBER AND HIGH FLAVOR

19 oz.	can chickpeas, drained & rinsed	540 mL
1	red pepper, diced OR 8 oz. (227 mL) jar of roasted red peppers, drained & chopped	1
10-12	kalamata olives (optional)	10-12
½	red onion, finely chopped	½
¼ cup	chopped fresh parsley	60 mL
3 tbsp.	fresh lemon juice	45 mL
2 tbsp.	olive oil	30 mL
1 tsp.	Dijon mustard	5 mL
2	garlic cloves, minced	2
	salt & pepper to taste	

- Combine all ingredients; refrigerate until serving – up to 24 hours.

VARIATIONS   Serve salad on a bed of mixed greens. Use half chickpeas and half lentils, black or kidney beans.

YIELD   **5 – 6 SERVINGS**

Lobster Caesar Salad, page 151
Lobster Bisque, page 71

Couscous Chickpea Salad

FRESH LEMON JUICE AND CUMIN MAKE A TANGY, EARTHY-TASTING DRESSING

1 tbsp.	butter	15 mL
3	garlic cloves, minced	3
1¼ cups	water	300 mL
1 cup	couscous	250 mL
½ tsp.	salt	2 mL
1 cup	chopped fresh parsley	250 mL
½	onion, finely chopped	½
2	Roma tomatoes, seeded, chopped	2
½	English cucumber, diced	½
2 cups	cooked chickpeas	500 mL
½ cup	crumbled feta cheese	125 mL
¼ cup	fresh lemon juice	60 mL
2 tbsp.	olive oil	30 mL
1½ tsp.	ground cumin	7 mL
1 tsp.	salt	5 mL
¼ tsp.	pepper	1 mL

- In a large saucepan, melt butter and sauté garlic. Add water; bring to a boil. Stir in couscous and salt. Remove from heat and cover. Let sit for 5 minutes, then stir with a fork. Cool.
- To couscous, add parsley, onion, tomatoes, cucumber, chickpeas and feta cheese.
- **For dressing**, combine lemon juice, oil, cumin, salt and pepper. Mix well. Toss lightly with couscous mixture.
- Refrigerate until ready to serve – up to 24 hours.

YIELD   *6 – 8 SERVINGS*

See photograph on page 87.

 A north-African staple, couscous is a granular pasta made from semolina (crushed durum wheat). It may be served with meat, vegetables and fruit as a main dish, salad or dessert. It is also served with milk as a type of porridge.

CLASSIC FOUR OR FIVE BEAN SALAD

A PERENNIAL PICNIC PARTNER WITH VERSATILE VARIATIONS

19 oz.	can kidney beans	540 mL
19 oz.	can garbanzo beans (chickpeas)	540 mL
19 oz.	can lima beans OR black beans (or both)	540 mL
19 oz.	can white beans (cannellini)	540 mL
1	onion, diced OR 1 cup (250 mL) sliced green onion	1
1	red OR green pepper, diced	1

RED WINE VINEGAR DRESSING:

⅓ cup	red wine vinegar	75 mL
⅓ cup	olive oil	75 mL
2	garlic cloves, minced	2
3 tbsp.	chopped fresh parsley	45 mL
1 tbsp.	chopped fresh basil OR thyme	15 mL
	salt & pepper to taste	
¼ cup	sugar (optional)	60 mL

- Rinse and drain beans. Combine beans with onions and peppers.
- **For dressing**, shake all ingredients together; pour over salad. Cover and refrigerate overnight.

VARIATIONS   Add 19 oz. (540 mL) can EACH green and yellow beans or add 2 cups (500 mL) EACH blanched fresh green or yellow beans. Add 12 oz. (341 mL) can of corn kernels.

Add 1 English cucumber, chopped. Add 1 tsp. (5 mL) Dijon mustard to the dressing. Substitute Splenda or another sugar replacement for the sugar.

For a Middle Eastern dressing try a **Cumin Vinaigrette**, ½ cup (125 mL) cider vinegar, 1 tbsp. (15 mL) Dijon mustard, 1½ tsp. (7 mL) ground cumin, 1 tsp. (5 mL) minced garlic, 1 tsp. (5 mL) freshly ground pepper, ½ tsp. (2 mL) salt, 1 cup (250 mL) olive oil. Combine all ingredients, except oil; whisk well. Slowly drizzle in oil, whisking until smooth.

YIELD   *10 – 12 SERVINGS*

PASTA PERFECTION

MEDITERRANEAN FLAVORS ARE PERFECT IN PASTA SALAD

1½ cups	dry small pasta (rotini, fusilli, etc.)	375 mL
2 tbsp.	olive oil	30 mL
1	head of broccoli, cut into florets	1
½	green OR red pepper, diced	½
1	garlic clove, minced	1
10-12	grape tomatoes	10-12
10-12	kalamata olives, pitted, chopped	10-12
3 tbsp.	extra-virgin olive oil	45 mL
2 tbsp.	red wine vinegar	30 mL
1 tsp.	dried basil	5 mL
⅓ cup	grated Parmesan cheese	75 mL
	freshly ground pepper	

- Cook pasta to "al dente" stage according to package directions. Drain, rinse and cool.
- In a skillet over medium-high heat, heat 2 tbsp. (30 mL) oil and sauté broccoli, pepper and garlic until broccoli is tender-crisp, 3-4 minutes.
- In a large bowl, combine pasta, sautéed vegetables, tomatoes and olives.
- **For dressing**, combine 3 tbsp. (45 mL) oil, vinegar and basil. Pour over salad; toss well. Toss Parmesan with salad. Add freshly ground pepper to taste.
- Serve immediately or refrigerate to serve later.

YIELD   *8 SERVINGS*

Pasta & Fresh Vegetable Salad

Pasta salads are staples at barbecues and picnics —
cider vinegar adds zesty flavor

Poppy Seed Dressing:

⅓ cup	sugar	75 mL
1 tsp.	salt	5 mL
⅓ cup	apple cider vinegar	75 mL
½	onion, chopped	½
2 tbsp.	poppy seeds	30 mL
⅔ cup	vegetable oil	150 mL
4 cups	cooked pasta (rotini, fusilli, macaroni)	1 L
1	red OR green pepper, chopped	1
2	carrots, thinly sliced	2
4	green onions, chopped	4
½	English cucumber, sliced	½
2 cups	chopped broccoli florets	500 mL
1 cup	grated Cheddar cheese	250 mL

- **For dressing**, in a blender, combine sugar, salt, vinegar, onion and poppy seeds. With the blender running, slowly pour in oil; blend thoroughly.
- In a large bowl, combine pasta, pepper, carrots, onion, cucumber and broccoli.
- Pour dressing over pasta and vegetables. Refrigerate for several hours or overnight.
- Just before serving, toss the cheese with the salad.

NOTE   Let pasta salads come to room temperature before serving. Taste and adjust the seasoning as the pasta (starch) absorbs flavors, sometimes making the salad too bland.

YIELD   *6 SERVINGS*

LAYERED PASTA SALAD

A SPECIAL MAKE-AHEAD TREAT FOR PASTA LOVERS!

3 cups	cooked pasta (rotini, fusilli, etc.)	750 mL
1 tbsp.	vegetable oil	15 mL
2 cups	shredded lettuce	500 mL
3	hard-boiled eggs, sliced	3
8 oz.	ham, cubed	250 g
10 oz.	frozen green peas, cooked & cooled	283 g
1 cup	shredded Monterey Jack cheese	250 mL
1 cup	mayonnaise	250 mL
½ cup	sour cream	125 mL
2 tsp.	Dijon mustard	10 mL
¼ cup	sliced green onions	60 mL
2 tbsp.	chopped fresh parsley	30 mL

- Toss pasta with oil.
- In a straight-sided glass bowl, layer pasta, lettuce, eggs, ham, peas and cheese.
- Combine mayonnaise, sour cream and mustard; spread over cheese.
- Sprinkle green onions and parsley on top.
- Chill for at least 6 hours before serving. This salad may be made a day ahead and refrigerated.

YIELD   *6 – 8 SERVING*

 To keep pasta from becoming too soft, cook it just to the al dente (firm to the bite) stage. Rinse with cold water to wash off excess starch and stop the cooking process. The pasta can then absorb dressing and still hold its shape. Taste salad before serving and adjust the seasoning as the pasta may have subdued the dressing flavors. Dressings/sauces with intense flavors are best for cold or hot pasta dishes. For hot pasta dishes, unrinsed hot pasta will absorb more sauce. Combine hot pasta immediately with hot sauce.

SPAGHETTI SALAD

READY-MADE DRESSING MAKES THIS FAST AND EASY

8 oz.	uncooked spaghetti	250 g
16 oz.	bottle of Italian dressing	500 mL
2	cucumbers, peeled & diced	2
2	tomatoes, diced	2
1	small red onion, chopped	1
1	green pepper, chopped	1
2 tbsp.	grated Parmesan cheese	30 mL
1 tbsp.	poppy seeds	15 mL
1 tbsp.	sesame seeds (optional)	15 mL
1 tbsp.	celery seed (optional)	15 mL
½ tsp.	EACH salt & pepper	2 mL

- Break spaghetti lengths into fourths. Cook according to package directions. Drain and cool. Marinate overnight in half the Italian dressing.
- Add remaining ingredients. Mix well.
- Refrigerate until ready to serve. Taste; add more dressing if needed.

YIELD   8 SERVINGS

WHEAT-BERRY SALAD

CRANBERRIES AND HERBS COMPLEMENT THE CHEWY TEXTURE OF WHEAT BERRIES

3 qts.	water	3 L
1 tbsp.	salt	15 mL
1 lb.	dried wheat berries*	500 g
¾ cup	dried cranberries	175 mL
⅓ cup	minced red onion	75 mL
⅓ cup	finely chopped fresh herbs (chives, chervil, tarragon, rosemary)	75 mL
¼ cup	raspberry vinegar	60 mL
2 tbsp.	olive oil	30 mL
	salt & pepper to taste	

WHEAT-BERRY SALAD

(CONTINUED)

- Bring water, salt and wheat berries to a boil in a large saucepan. Cook for 60 minutes, or until soft but chewy. Drain well.
- Combine wheat berries, cranberries, onion and herbs in a large bowl.
- Combine vinegar and oil. Whisk well.
- Pour dressing over salad and let sit, covered, 30 minutes to 2 hours. Add salt and pepper to taste. Serve at room temperature.

YIELD   *8 SERVINGS*

* See note on page 126.

WILD RICE SALAD

CHEWY NUTRITIOUS WILD RICE IN A COLORFUL SALAD

1½ cups	cooked wild rice	375 mL
1 cup	cooked long-grain rice	250 mL
4 oz.	sugar snap peas, halved crosswise	115 g
½	yellow or orange pepper, sliced, cut into 1" (2.5 cm) pieces	½
6	mushrooms, sliced	6
2	green onions, sliced	2
	salt & pepper to taste	

SOY SAUCE DRESSING:

¼ cup	olive oil	60 mL
2 tbsp.	soy sauce	30 mL
1 tsp.	finely grated lemon peel	5 mL
2 tsp.	finely grated fresh ginger	10 mL
1	garlic clove, minced	1

- In a medium salad bowl, combine all salad ingredients.
- **For dressing**, place all ingredients in a blender. Process thoroughly. Pour over rice mixture; toss lightly. Add salt and pepper to taste.

YIELD   *6 SERVINGS*

POTATO SALAD

A GREAT CARRY-ALONG FOR AN OUTDOOR PICNIC!

8	potatoes, cooked & cubed	8
4	hard-boiled eggs, peeled & diced	4
½ cup	chopped celery	125 mL
½ cup	chopped green pepper	125 mL
¼ cup	chopped green onion	60 mL
½ cup	chopped radish	125 mL
⅓ cup	mayonnaise	75 mL
1 tbsp.	prepared mustard	15 mL
2 tbsp.	vinegar	30 mL
1 tsp.	sugar	5 mL
1 tsp.	salt	5 mL
½ tsp.	pepper	2 mL
	parsley, chopped onion OR radish for garnish	

- In a large bowl, combine potatoes, eggs, celery, pepper, onion and radish.
- **For dressing**, blend remaining ingredients together, except for garnishes. Pour over vegetables and mix gently.
- Garnish with parsley, chopped onion or radish. Chill.

VARIATIONS   Add 1 tsp. (5 mL) dried mustard, or to taste, for added flavor.
Substitute 2 tbsp. (30 mL) sweet pickle juice for the vinegar.

YIELD   *10 SERVINGS*

 To prevent eggs from cracking while boiling, add a little salt or vinegar to the water.

Sweet Potato Salad

SWEET POTATO ADDS COLOR AND FLAVOR

1 lb.	Yukon Gold OR red potatoes, peeled & cubed	500 g
1 lb.	sweet potatoes, peeled & cubed	500 g
1-2 tbsp.	white OR red wine vinegar	15-30 mL
2-3 tbsp.	Dijon mustard	30-45 mL
	salt & pepper to taste	
¼ cup	olive oil	60 mL
¼ cup	finely chopped onion	60 mL
¼ cup	finely chopped red pepper	60 mL
¼ cup	crumbled crisp bacon	60 mL
2-3 tbsp.	finely chopped dill pickle	30-45 mL

- In a large saucepan, bring Yukon Gold potatoes to a boil. Once they are boiling, add sweet potatoes; simmer, covered, for 10-12 minutes, just until tender.
- Place potatoes in a large bowl; let cool.
- **For dressing**, in a separate bowl, whisk vinegar, mustard, salt and pepper together. Whisk in oil, pouring slowly.
- Pour dressing over potatoes; stir in onion, peppers, bacon and pickle. Serve warm or cold.

YIELD   *6 SERVINGS*

Native to Central America, sweet potatoes have been used for 10,000 years. Often mistakenly called "yams" the most popular sweet potato variety has a dark orange skin and moist orange flesh. With a low glycemic index, sweet potatoes have been labeled an "antidiabetic" food – they help stabilize blood sugar levels and lower insulin resistance. High in vitamins A, C and B6, they are also a good source of manganese, copper, biotin, vitamins B5 and B2, and dietary fiber. Do NOT refrigerate sweet potatoes. They can be stored in a cool, dark, dry place for up to 2 weeks.

German Potato Salad

AN UNFORGETTABLE EXPERIENCE WHEN SERVED WITH PORK
OR WITH HAM AND RED CABBAGE!

6	potatoes, peeled & cubed	6

BACON DRESSING:

6 slices	bacon	6 slices
½ cup	chopped onion	125 mL
¼ cup	chopped celery	60 mL
1	dill pickle, chopped	1
1 tbsp.	flour	15 mL
½ cup	water	125 mL
½ cup	vinegar	125 mL
½ tsp.	sugar	2 mL
½ tsp.	salt	2 mL
¼ tsp.	dry mustard	1 mL
¼ tsp.	paprika	1 mL
1 tbsp.	chopped fresh parsley	15 mL

- Cook potatoes in water in a saucepan until just tender. Drain; keep warm.
- **For dressing**, in a skillet, fry bacon until crisp. Remove and crumble. Reserve 2 tbsp. (30 mL) of drippings.
- In reserved drippings, sauté onion, celery and pickle. Stir in flour. Add water, vinegar, sugar, salt and mustard. Cook on medium heat until smooth and thickened. Add crumbled bacon.
- Pour dressing over warm potatoes. Stir to coat evenly.
- Sprinkle with paprika and parsley. Serve warm.

VARIATIONS   *French Potato Salad*: Omit Bacon Dressing and combine ¼ cup (60 mL) EACH chicken stock, white wine and olive oil, with 2 tbsp. (30 mL) EACH Dijon mustard, white wine vinegar and capers OR ½ cup (125 mL) halved kalamata OR niçoise olives. Stir in 4 green onions, chopped; add salt and pepper to taste. Pour over warm potatoes. Serve warm or chilled.

Italian Potato Salad: Omit Bacon Dressing and combine 6 tbsp. (90 mL) olive oil, ¼ cup (60 mL) lemon juice, 2 tbsp. (30 mL) capers, 1 tbsp. (15 mL) EACH chopped fresh rosemary and garlic, ½ cup (125 mL) chopped green or red onion, salt and pepper to taste. Pour over warm potatoes. Serve warm or chilled.

YIELD   *6 – 8 SERVINGS*

ROQUEFORT POTATO SALAD

BLUE OR BLEU – THIS CHEESY DRESSING IS DELICIOUS.
THIS SALAD IS EVEN BETTER THE NEXT DAY

OLIVE OIL & MUSTARD DRESSING:

½-⅔ cup	olive oil	125-150 mL
⅓ cup	cider vinegar	75 mL
¼ cup	minced onion	60 mL
1	garlic clove, crushed	1
1 tbsp.	chopped fresh parsley	15 mL
1 tbsp.	minced fresh chives	15 mL
1-2 tbsp.	Dijon mustard	15-30 mL
2 tsp.	honey	10 mL
1-2 tsp.	grated lemon zest	5-10 mL
3 lbs.	Yukon Gold OR red potatoes, cooked, peeled & cubed	1.5 kg
	salt & pepper to taste	
8 slices	crumbled crisp bacon	8 slices
½ cup	crumbled Roquefort cheese, or more to taste	125 mL
1-2	hard-boiled eggs, grated	1-2
¼ cup	finely chopped chives	60 mL

- **For dressing,** in a large bowl, whisk together all ingredients.
- Add warm cooked potatoes to dressing; toss well. Add salt and pepper to taste. Refrigerate, covered, until serving.
- Before serving, sprinkle salad with bacon, blue cheese, egg and chives.

VARIATIONS Substitute Gorgonzola or Danish Blue cheese for Roquefort, or try feta. Serve this salad on plates garnished with butter lettuce or romaine.

YIELD . *8 SERVINGS*

ROASTED RED PEPPER POTATO SALAD

COLORFUL, WITH A LEMONY, CREAMY DRESSING.

3 lbs.	Yukon Gold potatoes, cooked & cubed	1.5 kg
2 tbsp.	white wine vinegar	30 mL
3 tbsp.	fresh lemon juice	45 mL

MAYO-MUSTARD DRESSING:

1 cup	finely chopped onion	250 mL
1 cup	mayonnaise	250 mL
½ cup	sour cream	125 mL
3 tbsp.	chopped fresh parsley	45 mL
2 tbsp.	Dijon mustard	30 mL
½-¾ cup	finely chopped, roasted red peppers	125-175 mL
½ cup	crumbled crisp bacon (optional)	125 mL
	salt & pepper to taste	

- Place warm potatoes in a large bowl. Toss gently with vinegar and lemon juice. Cool to room temperature.
- **For dressing**, in a small bowl, whisk all ingredients. Pour over potatoes.
- Toss red peppers and bacon gently with potatoes. Add salt and pepper.
- Refrigerate, covered, until ready to serve.

YIELD   6 SERVINGS

POTATO SALAD WITH SPICY SAUSAGE

HOT SAUSAGE ADDS VARIETY TO THIS SOUTHERN POTATO SALAD.

10 oz.	andouille, chorizo OR spicy Italian sausages, cut in bite-sized pieces	285 g
3 lbs.	potatoes, peeled, cooked & cubed	1.5 kg
3 tbsp.	white wine vinegar	45 mL
1-2 tbsp.	hot pepper sauce	15-30 mL
1-2 tbsp.	whole-grain Dijon mustard	15-30 mL
1	red OR green pepper, chopped	
1 cup	EACH chopped celery & red onion	150 mL
¼ cup	olive oil	60 mL
	salt & pepper to taste	

POTATO SALAD WITH SPICY SAUSAGE

(CONTINUED)

- In a large skillet over medium-high heat, sauté sausages until brown, about 5 minutes. Drain well.
- Whisk vinegar, pepper sauce and mustard in a large bowl. Add warm potatoes and toss gently. Gently stir in sausages, red peppers, celery, onions and oil. Add salt and pepper to taste. Serve warm or at room temperature.

YIELD   *6 – 8 SERVINGS*

POTATO SALAD WITH HERBS & LEMON-OLIVE OIL DRESSING

LEMON AND MINT ADD EXTRA ZEST TO THIS LOVELY POTATO SALAD

2 lbs.	potatoes, peeled, cooked & cubed	1 kg
¼ cup	olive oil	60 mL
½ cup	finely chopped red onion	125 mL
½ cup	finely-chopped red pepper OR roasted red pepper	125 mL
¼ cup	fresh lemon juice	60 mL
3 tbsp.	chopped fresh oregano OR basil	45 mL
2 tbsp.	chopped fresh parsley	30 mL
2 tbsp.	chopped fresh mint	30 mL
2 tsp.	salt	10 mL
¾ tsp.	freshly ground black pepper	3 mL

- Place warm potatoes in a large bowl. Add oil and toss well.
- Stir in onion, pepper, lemon juice, oregano, parsley, mint, salt and pepper. Cover and chill. Let stand at room temperature for 1 hour before serving.

VARIATION   ***Potato Salad with Anchovies***: Add ½ oz. (15 g) can of anchovies, chopped, and 4 green onions, chopped. Substitute red wine vinegar for lemon juice.

YIELD   *6 SERVINGS*

SALADE NIÇOISE

THE FLAVORS OF PROVENCE IN A HEARTY POTATO-TUNA SALAD – A CLASSIC

DIJON GARLIC DRESSING:

3 tbsp.	red wine vinegar	45 mL
2 tsp.	Dijon mustard	10 mL
2	garlic cloves, minced	2
	salt & freshly ground pepper to taste	
6 tbsp.	extra-virgin olive oil	90 mL
6	new red potatoes, cooked & quartered	6
1 lb.	green beans, steamed until tender-crisp	500 g
1 head	romaine, Boston or leaf lettuce	1 head
2	large ripe tomatoes, each in 8 wedges	2
½	EACH red & yellow pepper, in thin strips	½
5	hard-boiled eggs, quartered lengthwise	5
6 oz.	can tuna, drained & flaked	170 g
½ cup	Niçoise OR black Greek olives	125 mL
¼ cup	finely chopped fresh parsley	60 mL
2 tbsp.	capers	30 mL
8-10	anchovy fillets, chopped	8-10
	salt & freshly ground pepper to taste	

- **For dressing**, in a small bowl, combine vinegar, mustard, garlic, salt and pepper. Whisk in oil.
- In a large bowl, toss potatoes and beans with ¼ cup (60 mL) dressing.
- Arrange lettuce on a large platter. Top with potatoes and beans. Arrange tomatoes, peppers, eggs and tuna over top. Drizzle with remaining dressing. Top with olives, parsley, capers, anchovies, salt and pepper.

VARIATIONS   Substitute grilled fresh tuna or salmon for canned tuna.

Add ¼ cup (60 mL) EACH chopped fresh tarragon and chervil to dressing. Try cider vinegar or lemon juice instead of red wine vinegar.

Substitute asparagus for the green beans.

YIELD   *4 – 6 SERVINGS*

MELON & CHICKEN SALAD

A GREAT CHOICE FOR A LADIES' LUNCHEON

LEMON YOGURT DRESSING:

½ cup	plain yogurt	125 mL
⅓ cup	mayonnaise	75 mL
3 tbsp.	lemon juice	45 mL
½ tsp.	salt	2 mL
½ tsp.	pepper	2 mL
2 cups	diced cooked chicken	500 mL
1 cup	diced cantaloupe melon	250 mL
1 cup	diced honeydew melon	250 mL
½ cup	chopped celery	125 mL
2	green onions, chopped	2
	a variety of lettuce leaves	
	kale (optional)	
½ cup	cashews (optional)	125 mL
	blueberries	
	paprika	

- **For dressing**, in a small bowl, combine all ingredients.
- Combine the chicken, melon, celery and onions.
- Add enough of the dressing to just coat the chicken mixture. Refrigerate for an hour before serving.
- Serve salad on greens. Garnish with cashews, blueberries and paprika.

NOTE   The yogurt dressing may be used on other fruit salads or as a fruit dip. Omit the salt and pepper and add 1 tbsp. (15 mL) of honey.

YIELD   ***4 SERVINGS/1 CUP (250 ML) OF DRESSING***

TACO SALAD

A TASTY MEAL-IN-ONE SALAD

1 lb.	lean ground beef	500 g
1	head lettuce	1
1 lb.	Cheddar cheese, grated	500 g
2	green onions, chopped	2
2 stalks	celery, chopped	2 stalks
12	ripe olives, sliced	12
2	tomatoes, cubed	2
8 oz.	bottle of green onion dressing	250 mL
¼ cup	taco seasoning mix*	60 mL
8 oz.	bag taco-flavored tortilla chips, crushed	240 g

- In a skillet, sauté beef until well-browned. Drain off fat.
- Tear lettuce into bite-sized pieces.
- In a large mixing bowl, combine beef, lettuce, cheese, onions, celery, olives and tomatoes.
- In a small bowl, combine green onion dressing and taco seasoning mix. Add to beef and vegetables and toss until well mixed.
- When ready to serve add tortilla chips. Mix lightly and serve.

NOTE   * Use the Taco Seasoning Mix on page 95 or use a commercial mix.

YIELD   **6 SERVINGS**

Curried Cauliflower & Apple Soup, page 32
Onion Cheddar Shortcake, page 184
Springtime Salad, page 131

SUPERB FRENCH DRESSING

TANGY AND SWEET – THE NAME SAYS IT ALL

1 cup	ketchup	250 mL
¼ cup	sugar	60 mL
½ cup	herb-flavored vinegar	125 mL
1 tsp.	salt	5 mL
1	small onion, quartered	1
2	garlic cloves, peeled	2
½ tsp.	celery seed	2 mL
¼ tsp.	paprika	1 mL
¾ cup	olive or vegetable oil	175 mL

• Place all ingredients in a blender; blend for 1 minute.

YIELD   *3 CUPS (750 ML)*

THOUSAND ISLAND DRESSING

NOW YOU CAN MAKE THIS MUCH-LOVED DRESSING AT HOME

1 cup	mayonnaise	250 mL
2 tbsp.	chopped onion	30 mL
¾ cup	diced celery	175 mL
¼ cup	EACH stuffed olives, sweet pickle relish & chili sauce	60 mL
3 sprigs	fresh parsley	3 sprigs
2 tbsp.	chopped green pepper	30 mL
1	hard-boiled egg, quartered (optional)	1
1 tsp.	paprika	5 mL
	salt & pepper to taste	

• Place all ingredients in a blender. Blend until solids are finely chopped.

YIELD   *3½ CUPS (875 ML)*

Yogurt Herb Dressing

A MULTI-PURPOSE FLAVORFUL BLEND

½ cup	plain yogurt	125 mL
½ cup	mayonnaise	125 mL
¼ cup	milk	60 mL
½ tsp.	sugar	2 mL
½ tsp.	salt	2 mL
¼ tsp.	EACH dried oregano, dillweed & basil	1 mL

- Combine all ingredients. Blend well. Chill.
- Serve on tossed green salads or as a topping for baked potatoes.

YIELD   *1 CUP (250 ML)*

Cooked Salad Dressing

OLD-FASHIONED COOKED MAYONNAISE-TYPE DRESSING WITH A ZING!

1 tsp.	salt	5 mL
2 tsp.	dry mustard	10 mL
1 cup	sugar	250 mL
1 tsp.	paprika	5 mL
½ tsp.	pepper	2 mL
2 tbsp.	all-purpose flour	30 mL
2	eggs, beaten	2
1 cup	vinegar	250 mL
1 cup	milk, scalded	250 mL
1 tsp.	butter	5 mL

- In a saucepan, combine dry ingredients.
- Combine eggs with vinegar. Add to dry ingredients. Mix well.
- Add scalded milk. Bring to a boil. Reduce heat and cook for 10-12 minutes, or until thickened and smooth.
- Add butter. Continue to cook for an additional 2 minutes.

SERVING   Use on macaroni and potato salads. To use on green salads, thin with
SUGGESTIONS   cream. This is an excellent accompaniment to cold cuts.

YIELD   *2 CUPS (500 ML)*

BISCUITS & BREADS

Close your eyes and imagine the smell
of baking bread, nothing can compare
with the aroma of grandma's kitchen
on baking day. Homemade biscuits
and breads hot from the oven
make any meal a feast.

GARLIC CHEDDAR LOAF

THE PERFECT ACCOMPANIMENT FOR A BARBECUE!

1	loaf French bread	1
¾ cup	butter	175 mL
2 cups	grated Cheddar cheese	500 mL
¼ cup	sour cream	60 mL
3	garlic cloves, crushed	3
1 tbsp.	chopped fresh parsley	15 mL
1 tbsp.	chopped fresh dill	15 mL

- Slice the French loaf in half lengthwise.
- In a bowl, combine the remaining ingredients. Mix well.
- Spread cheese mixture over the 2 halves of bread. Place bread on a cookie sheet. Bake at 350°F (180°C) for 12 minutes, or until bubbly.
- Slice crosswise. Serve warm.

YIELD   1 LOAF

LEMON YOGURT SCONES

LIGHT AND VERY LEMONY, THESE SCONES ARE IDEAL FOR A SUMMER LUNCH OR DINNER WITH A FRUIT AND GREENS SALAD

2 cups	all-purpose flour	500 mL
2 tbsp.	sugar	30 mL
1 tbsp.	baking powder	15 mL
½ tsp.	baking soda	2 mL
½ tsp.	salt	2 mL
½ cup	cold margarine OR butter	125 mL
1 cup	plain yogurt	250 mL
1 tbsp.	grated lemon rind	15 mL

Lemon Yogurt Scones

(Continued)

- In a mixing bowl, combine the flour, sugar, baking powder, baking soda and salt. With a pastry blender, cut in the butter until crumbly.
- Combine the yogurt and lemon rind. Stir into dry ingredients. Mix until just moistened. Form into a ball.
- Turn dough onto a lightly floured board. Flatten to 1" (2.5 cm) thickness. With a floured cookie cutter, cut out scones. Place on an ungreased cookie sheet.
- Bake at 425°F (220°C) for 12-14 minutes, or until lightly browned.

VARIATIONS   Omit lemon rind and add 1 tbsp. (15 mL) of freshly chopped dill or ¼ cup (60 mL) of grated sharp cheese.

YIELD   **1 DOZEN SCONES**

Sour Cream Biscuits

Quick and Easy – Make While the Soup is Simmering

1¼ cups	all-purpose flour	300 mL
2 tsp.	baking powder	10 mL
½ tsp.	salt	2 mL
¼ tsp.	baking soda	1 mL
½ cup	sour cream	125 mL
¼ cup	milk	60 mL

- In a mixing bowl, combine flour, baking powder, salt and baking soda.
- In a small bowl, combine sour cream and milk.
- Make a well in center of dry ingredients; add milk mixture. Stir just until dough clings together and forms a ball.
- On a lightly floured surface, knead dough lightly. Roll out onto ⅓" (1 cm) thickness. With a biscuit cutter, cut into 1¼" (3 cm) rounds. Transfer to a lightly greased baking sheet.
- Bake at 375°F (190°C) for 15 minutes, or until golden.

YIELD   **8 BISCUITS**

See photograph on page 105.

BUTTERMILK BISCUITS

THESE LIGHT, FLUFFY BISCUITS ARE GREAT WITH A BOWL OF HOT SOUP!

3 cups	all-purpose flour	750 mL
1½ tsp.	salt	7 mL
4 tsp.	baking powder	20 mL
½ tsp.	baking soda	2 mL
⅓ cup	vegetable shortening OR butter	75 mL
1½ cups	buttermilk	375 mL

- Sift flour, salt, baking powder and baking soda into a mixing bowl.
- With a pastry blender, cut shortening into dry ingredients.
- Add buttermilk all at once; stir in only until dry ingredients are moistened.
- Turn dough out onto a lightly floured surface. With a minimum of handling, flatten dough to 1" (2.5 cm) thickness. With a floured 2" (5 cm) biscuit cutter, cut out biscuits; place on a parchment-paper-lined baking sheet.
- Let biscuits stand at room temperature for 15 minutes.
- Bake at 350°F (180°C) for 15-20 minutes, or until just lightly browned.

VARIATIONS   Biscuits are infinitely versatile – you may add herbs and cheeses to the dry ingredients; try ¼ cup (60 mL) minced green onion or chives OR 1 tsp. (5 mL) dried Italian seasoning, parsley, rosemary or oregano; try ½ cup (125 mL) grated Parmesan OR up to 1 cup (250 mL) grated sharp Cheddar. Cayenne pepper or minced jalapeño add extra zip with the Cheddar. With the liquid ingredients, you may add up to ½ cup (125 mL) cooked sausage or ham.

YIELD   *16 – 20 BISCUITS*

BAKING POWER BISCUITS

LIGHT AND FLUFFY, THESE BISCUITS ARE PERFECT WITH SOUPS AND SALADS

2 cups	all-purpose flour	500 mL
4 tsp.	baking powder	20 mL
1 tbsp.	sugar	15 mL
½ tsp.	salt	2 mL
½ cup	shortening	125 mL
¾ cup	milk	175 mL
1	egg, beaten	1

- In a mixing bowl, combine flour, baking powder, sugar and salt.
- With a pastry blender, cut shortening into dry ingredients until mixture is the consistency of coarse meal.
- Combine milk and egg. Add gradually to blended mixture to form a soft dough. Knead until well mixed. Chill for 1-3 hours.
- Turn dough out onto a floured surface. Roll out ¾" (2 cm) thick. Cut out circles with a floured cutter. Place on a greased cookie sheet.
- Bake at 450°F (230°C) for 10-12 minutes.

VARIATIONS For **Herb Biscuits**, add 2 tbsp. mixed herbs, parsley, basil, oregano, etc. to biscuit dough.

For **Cheese Biscuits**, add ½-1 cup (125-250 mL) grated sharp Cheddar cheese and a sprinkle of cayenne pepper, omit sugar.

YIELD **12 BISCUITS**

 If biscuit dough is kneaded inside a large plastic bag it won't stick to hands and it won't dry out when left to chill.

ONION CHEDDAR SHORTCAKE

SERVE THESE FLAVORFUL SQUARES WARM WITH A HEARTY BOWL OF SOUP

1 tbsp.	olive oil	15 mL
1 tbsp.	butter	15 mL
3	medium onions, sliced	3
1 cup	all-purpose flour	250 mL
2 tsp.	baking powder	10 mL
¼ tsp.	salt	1 mL
3 tbsp.	butter	45 mL
½ cup	milk	125 mL
1 cup	grated Cheddar cheese	250 mL
1	egg	1
1 cup	milk	250 mL
1 tsp.	prepared mustard	5 mL

- In a skillet, heat oil and 1 tbsp. (15 mL) butter. Sauté onions until translucent.
- In a mixing bowl, combine flour, baking powder and salt. With a pastry blender, cut in 3 tbsp. (45 mL) butter until crumbly. Add ½ cup (125 mL) milk; stir only until moistened. Press batter into a lightly greased 9" (23 cm) square pan.
- Spread cooked onions over batter. Sprinkle cheese over onions.
- In a small bowl, combine egg, 1 cup (250 mL) milk and mustard. Pour over cheese.
- Bake at 450°F (230°C) for 8 minutes. Reduce heat to 350°F (180°C) and bake an additional 20 minutes.
- Cut into squares and serve warm.

VARIATION   For **Herbed Onion Cheddar Shortcake**, add 1 tbsp. (15 mL) dried Italian herbs to the dry ingredients.

YIELD   *9 SERVINGS*

See photograph on page 175.

PEPPER CORN BREAD

WHAT A GREAT COMBINATION WITH CHILI OR STEW!

1 cup	melted butter	250 mL
¾ cup	buttermilk	175 mL
1½ cups	creamed corn	375 mL
1 cup	cornmeal	250 mL
1	large onion, chopped	1
2	eggs, beaten	2
½ tsp.	baking soda	2 mL
1½ cups	grated sharp Cheddar cheese	375 mL
3	hot peppers, chopped	3

- In a mixing bowl, combine butter, buttermilk, corn, cornmeal, onion, egg and baking soda until well blended.
- Pour half the batter into a greased 9" (23 cm) square pan.
- Sprinkle with half the cheese, all the peppers, then remaining cheese.
- Pour remaining batter on top.
- Bake at 350°F (180°C) for 50 minutes.
- Serve warm or cold.

VARIATIONS   Use jalapeño peppers or combine with other hot peppers.

YIELD   **10 BISCUITS**

 When preparing hot peppers, wear rubber gloves as the juices irritate the skin and eyes. Don't rub your eyes.

JOHNNY CAKE

ORIGINALLY CALLED "JOURNEY CAKE", THIS CORNMEAL BREAD IS DELICIOUS
SERVED WARM WITH SYRUP OR COLD WITH HONEY

1 cup	cornmeal	250 mL
½ cup	milk	125 mL
½ cup	shortening	125 mL
½ cup	sugar	125 mL
1⅓ cups	all-purpose flour	325 mL
2½ tsp.	baking powder	12 mL
1 tsp.	salt	5 mL
1	egg	1
1 cup	milk	250 mL

- Combine cornmeal and milk. Set aside.
- In another bowl, cream shortening and blend in sugar.
- Combine flour, baking powder and salt.
- Mix together egg and milk.
- Add dry ingredients, alternately with liquids, to creamed mixture.
- Blend in cornmeal mixture.
- Pour batter into a greased 9" (23 cm) square pan; bake at 350°F (180°C) for 40-45 minutes.
- Serve warm with butter, maple syrup, pancake or fruit syrups or honey.

VARIATION   For **Cheese Corn Bread**, sprinkle ½-1 cup (125-250 mL) of grated sharp Cheddar cheese on top of batter.

For **Corn Muffins**, divide batter between 12 medium muffin cups and bake at 425°F (220°C) for 12 minutes.

YIELD   ***9 SERVINGS***

OATMEAL BUTTERMILK LOAF

SERVE WITH A CHILLED FRUIT SOUP OR A FRESH FRUIT SALAD

½ cup	sugar	125 mL
⅓ cup	liquid honey	75 mL
¼ cup	butter, melted	60 mL
1	egg	1
1½ cups	all-purpose flour	375 mL
1 tsp.	baking soda	5 mL
1 tsp.	baking powder	5 mL
¼ tsp.	salt	1 mL
¾ cup	quick rolled oats	175 mL
1 cup	buttermilk	250 mL
½ cup	raisins	125 mL

- In a large mixing bowl, beat together sugar, honey, butter and egg.
- In a small bowl, combine flour, baking soda, baking powder and salt. Add oats; mix well.
- Gradually add dry ingredients to butter mixture alternately with buttermilk. Stir in raisins.
- Pour batter into a greased 5 x 9" (13 x 23 cm) loaf pan.
- Bake at 350°F (180°C) for 50 minutes, or until a skewer inserted in the center comes out clean.
- Cool on a wire rack for 5 minutes. Turn out of loaf pan. Let cool completely.

YIELD   *1 LOAF*

CHEESE BREAD

TRY THIS CHEESE AND HERB BREAD WITH YOUR FAVORITE SOUPS

1	egg, well beaten	1
1 cup	milk	250 mL
1 tbsp.	melted butter	15 mL
2 cups	all-purpose flour	500 mL
4 tsp.	baking powder	20 mL
1 tbsp.	sugar	15 mL
½ tsp.	onion salt	2 mL
¼ tsp.	garlic powder	1 mL
½ tsp.	oregano	2 mL
¼ tsp.	dry mustard	1 mL
1¼ cups	grated sharp Cheddar cheese	300 mL
1 tbsp.	chopped dill OR parsley (optional)	15 mL

- In a small bowl, combine egg, milk and butter.
- In a mixing bowl, combine remaining ingredients. Make a well in dry ingredients and add milk mixture. Stir until well blended.
- Pour batter into a greased 5 x 9" (2 L) loaf pan.
- Bake at 350°F (180°C) for 45 minutes.

YIELD   12 – 15 SLICES

ONION & CHEESE BREAD

SERVE WARM WITH A BOWL OF CHILI OR WITH TACO SOUP, PAGE 95. SUPERB!

½ cup	chopped onion	125 mL
1 tbsp.	butter OR margarine	15 mL
1½ cups	all-purpose flour	375 mL
1 tbsp.	baking powder	15 mL
½ tsp.	salt	2 mL
3 tbsp.	butter	45 mL
1 cup	grated sharp Cheddar cheese	250 mL
1	egg, beaten	1
½ cup	milk	125 mL

ONION & CHEESE BREAD

(CONTINUED)

- In a small skillet, fry onion in butter until translucent. Set aside.
- In a mixing bowl, combine flour, baking powder and salt. Cut in butter until mixture is crumbly. Stir in ½ of the cheese.
- In a small bowl, combine egg, milk and onion mixture. Add to flour mixture. Mix. Pat soft dough into a greased 5 x 9" (13 x 23 cm) loaf pan or 8" (20 cm) round pan. Sprinkle with the remaining half of the cheese.
- Bake at 400°F (200°C) for 25 minutes, or until golden brown.

YIELD   *1 LOAF*

ONION BEER BREAD

A TASTY LOAF TOPPED WITH CRISPY ONION RINGS

2¾ cups	all-purpose flour	675 mL
1 tbsp.	baking powder	15 mL
1 tbsp.	sugar	15 mL
2 tsp.	dry mustard	10 mL
½ tsp.	salt	2 mL
1 cup	grated sharp Cheddar cheese	250 mL
2 tsp.	dried crushed basil	10 mL
12 oz.	beer (1 can)	355 mL
1	small onion, thinly sliced into rings	1
¼ cup	grated sharp Cheddar cheese	60 mL

- In a large bowl, stir together flour, baking powder, sugar, mustard and salt. Mix in 1 cup (250 mL) of cheese and the basil. Stir in beer, mixing until dry ingredients are moistened.
- Pat soft dough into a greased 5 x 9" (13 x 23 cm) loaf pan. Arrange onion rings on top of batter. Sprinkle with remaining cheese.
- Bake at 350°F (180°C) for 45 minutes, or until golden. Let stand for 5 minutes before removing from pan. Let cool a bit before slicing.

YIELD   *1 LOAF (12 – 16 SLICES)*

HERBED BEER BREAD

A QUICK FLAVORFUL BREAD THAT IS EASY FOR ANYONE TO MAKE

2¾ cups	all-purpose flour	675 mL
2 tbsp.	sugar	30 mL
2 tbsp.	baking powder	30 mL
1 tsp.	salt	5 mL
¼ tsp.	oregano	1 mL
¼ tsp.	thyme	1 mL
¼ tsp.	dried dillweed	1 mL
12 oz.	beer (1 can)	355 mL
	butter	

- In a large bowl, stir together the first 7 ingredients.
- Add beer. Mix well.
- Place batter in a 4 x 8" (10 x 20 cm) greased loaf pan.
- Bake at 375°F (190°C) for 50 minutes, or until golden on top. Brush the top with butter.
- Let stand in pan for 5 minutes before turning out onto a cooling rack.

NOTE   Beer Bread mix makes a nice gift from the kitchen. Combine the first 7 ingredients. Place in an airtight container. Include directions for adding beer and baking. Decorate container with gift wrap or leftover fabric and ribbons or bows.

YIELD   *1 LOAF*

TOMATO BASIL BREAD

THIS SAVORY LOAF IS IDEAL SERVED WITH SOUPS, SALADS OR MAIN COURSES

½ cup	butter	125 mL
1 tbsp.	tomato paste	15 mL
1 tbsp.	brown sugar	15 mL
2	eggs	2
2 cups	all-purpose flour	500 mL
1 tsp.	EACH baking powder & baking soda	5 mL
1 tsp.	crumbled dried basil	5 mL
½ cup	tomato juice	125 mL
1 cup	grated Cheddar cheese	250 mL

TOMATO BASIL BREAD

(CONTINUED)

- In a mixing bowl, beat butter, tomato paste, sugar and eggs until fluffy.
- In a small bowl, combine flour, baking powder, baking soda and basil.
- Gradually add dry ingredients to butter mixture alternately with tomato juice. Fold in cheese.
- Spread batter in a greased 5 x 9" (13 x 22 cm) loaf pan.
- Bake at 350°F (180°C) for 45 minutes, or until a skewer inserted in the center comes out clean.
- Cool on a wire rack for 5 minutes. Turn out of loaf pan. Let cool completely. Wrap and refrigerate for 12 hours before serving.

YIELD   *1 LOAF*

WHOLE-WHEAT SODA BREAD

SERVE THIS HEARTY, COARSE-TEXTURED LOAF WITH SOUPS AND STEWS

1 cup	all-purpose flour	250 mL
1 tsp.	EACH baking powder & baking soda	5 mL
½ tsp.	salt	2 mL
2 tbsp.	sugar	30 mL
2 cups	whole-wheat flour	500 mL
1½ cups	buttermilk	375 mL
1 tbsp.	melted butter	15 mL

- In a large mixing bowl, combine the all-purpose flour, baking powder, baking soda, salt and sugar. Add the whole-wheat flour. Mix well.
- Add buttermilk. Mix only until dry ingredients are moistened.
- Turn dough onto a floured surface. Knead gently for about 2 minutes, or until dough is smooth and ingredients are well mixed.
- Shape dough into a ball. Place on a lightly greased cookie sheet. Shape dough into a 7-8" (18-20 cm) circle about 1½" (4 cm) in height.
- With the use of a floured knife, mark the circle of dough into quarters by cutting halfway through to the bottom.
- Bake at 375°F (190°C) for 40 minutes, or until the loaf sounds hollow when tapped.
- Brush top of bread with melted butter. Cool on a wire rack.

YIELD   *1 LOAF*

OVERNIGHT BUNS

HERE IS A SOLUTION FOR BUSY BAKERS
WHO LIKE TO SERVE THEIR FAMILIES HOME-BAKED BUNS

1 tbsp.	yeast (not fast-rising)	15 mL
1 tsp.	sugar	5 mL
½ cup	warm water	125 mL
1 cup	vegetable oil	250 mL
1 tbsp.	salt	15 mL
½ cup	sugar	125 mL
2	eggs	2
3 cups	warm water	750 mL
11 cups	all-purpose flour	2.6 L
1	egg	1
¼ cup	milk	60 mL

- Soak yeast and 1 tsp. (5 mL) sugar in water for 10 minutes, or until risen.
- Beat together oil, salt, sugar and eggs.
- Add yeast mixture and warm water. Beat well.
- Add half of the flour and beat well. Knead in remaining flour.
- Place dough in a large greased bowl; cover with a tea towel; let rise for about 2 hours, or until double in size.
- Punch down dough; cover; let rise again.
- Shape dough into buns the size of golf balls. Place on greased cookie sheets. Cover and let rise overnight.
- In the morning brush buns with a mixture of 1 egg and ¼ cup (60 mL) milk.
- Bake at 375°F (190°C) for 20 minutes, or until golden brown.

YIELD   *8 DOZEN BUNS THAT FREEZE VERY WELL*

WHITE BREAD

SERVE WARM AND BUTTERED WITH A HEARTY BOWL OF SOUP

1 tsp.	sugar	5 mL
½ cup	warm water	125 mL
1 tbsp.	yeast (1 envelope, 7 g)	15 mL
1½ cups	water	375 mL
½ cup	milk	125 mL
3 tbsp.	butter OR margarine	45 mL
3 tbsp.	sugar	45 mL
2 tsp.	salt	10 mL
1	egg, beaten	1
7 cups	all-purpose flour	1.75 L
1	egg	1
1 tbsp.	water	15 mL

- In a large bowl, dissolve 1 tsp. (5 mL) sugar in ½ cup (125 mL) warm water. Sprinkle yeast over. Let sit for 8 minutes.
- In a saucepan, combine 1½ cups (375 mL) water, milk and margarine. Warm over low heat until margarine melts. Add to yeast mixture.
- Stir in 3 tbsp. (45 mL) sugar, salt and egg. Add 2 cups (500 mL) of flour. Beat until smooth.
- Gradually add remaining flour until a soft dough forms.
- Turn dough out onto a floured surface. Knead until smooth and elastic.
- Place dough in a large greased bowl. Cover and let rise until double in size, about 1 hour. Punch down and let rise again. Punch down and let rest for 15 minutes.
- Shape into loaves. Place in greased loaf pans. Let rise until double in size. Brush loaves with a mixture of 1 egg and 1 tbsp. (15 mL) of water.
- Bake at 375°F (190°C) for 40-45 minutes, or until golden brown. Turn out on wire racks to cool.

YIELD   *3 MEDIUM LOAVES OR 2 LARGE LOAVES*

TRADITIONAL FRENCH BREAD

CRISP CRUST AND MOIST CHEWY CENTER – HEAVENLY!

3 cups	all-purpose flour	750 mL
2 cups	warm water	500 mL
1 tbsp.	sugar	15 mL
1 tsp.	salt	5 mL
2 tbsp.	vegetable oil	30 mL
2 tbsp.	instant yeast	30 mL
2-2½ cups	all-purpose flour	500-625 mL
	cornmeal	
	water	

- In an electric mixer, with a dough hook, combine flour, water, sugar, salt and oil. Mix in yeast. Gradually add remaining flour until the dough comes away from the sides of the bowl. Knead for 8-9 minutes, or until the dough is smooth and pliable.
- Shape dough into a ball and place in a large well-greased bowl. Cover and let rise in a warm place until doubled in volume, about 30 minutes.
- Turn dough out onto a greased surface, divide in half and form into 2 loaves. Place loaves into a greased and cornmeal-sprinkled 2-loaf French loaf pan (or 2 large baking pans). Make 4-5 diagonal slashes along top of loaves. Let rise until doubled.
- Mist loaves with water. Bake on the middle rack at 375°F (190°C) with a pan of water on the lower rack. After baking for 10 minutes, mist again with water and continue to bake until golden brown. Baked loaves should sound hollow when tapped.

YIELD   2 LOAVES

 Slashing the tops of loaves before baking assists in the rising of the dough. Misting loaves while baking creates steam which produces a crisp hard crust. French bread and baguette pans vary, depending on the width of the desired loaves. They look like joined half tubes. Baguette pans are 2-3" (5-8 cm) wide and 15-17" (38-43 cm) long. Very thin loaves are called *ficelles* (strings), and are baked in special pans.

WHOLE-WHEAT BREAD/BUNS

A WHOLE ORANGE ADDED TO WHOLE-WHEAT BREAD KEEPS THE BREAD MOIST
AND GIVES A PLEASANT AROMA WHILE BAKING

½ cup	mashed potatoes	125 mL
½ cup	butter OR margarine	125 mL
⅓ cup	sugar	75 mL
2 cups	scalded milk, cooled to room temperature	500 mL
2	eggs	2
1 tsp.	baking powder	5 mL
½ tsp.	salt	2 mL
½ tsp.	baking soda	2 mL
¼ cup	honey	60 mL
1	orange (seed orange; chop, rind & all, in a food processor)	1
2 cups	all-purpose flour	500 mL
2 tbsp.	instant yeast (2 envelopes, 2 x 7g)	30 mL
5-6 cups	whole-wheat flour	1.25-1.5 L
1	egg	1
1 tbsp.	water	15 mL

- In a large bowl combine potatoes, margarine, sugar and milk. Mix well.
- Add eggs, baking powder, salt, soda, honey and orange. Mix well.
- In a small bowl combine the white flour and yeast. Add to the milk mixture. Beat well.
- Add the whole-wheat flour, 1 cup (250 mL) at a time, mixing well after each addition. When batter becomes too stiff to mix, remove from bowl and knead on a floured surface. Continue to add flour until dough comes away from hands and becomes smooth. Grease bowl and return dough to it. Grease top of dough. Cover with a clean tea towel.
- Let rise in a warm place until double in bulk, about 1 hour.
- Knead down. Shape into loaves, mini-loaves or buns. Place in greased baking pans. Let rise in a warm place until double in bulk. For a shiny crust, brush tops with an egg and water mixture, after dough rises.
- Bake at 350°F (180°C), about 30 minutes for loaves, 15-20 minutes for mini loaves and buns, or until the crust sounds hollow.

YIELD   *3, 5 X 9" (2 L) LOAVES, OR 20, 2½ X 4" (6 X 10 CM) MINI LOAVES*

RYE BREAD

A GREAT BASE FOR A GRILLED REUBEN SANDWICH!

1 cup	warm milk	250 mL
1 cup	warm water	250 mL
2 tbsp.	honey	30 mL
2 tbsp.	vegetable oil	30 mL
2 tsp.	salt	10 mL
2 cups	dark rye flour	500 mL
1 tbsp.	wheat gluten	15 mL
1 tbsp.	instant yeast	15 mL
2½-3 cups	all-purpose flour	625-750 mL

- In an electric mixer, with a dough hook, combine milk, water, honey, oil, salt, rye flour and wheat gluten. Mix in yeast.
- Gradually add remaining flour until dough comes away from the sides of the bowl. Knead for 8 minutes, or until dough is smooth and elastic.
- Place dough in a greased bowl. Cover and let rise in a warm place until doubled in volume.
- Turn dough onto an oiled surface; divide into 2 portions and form loaves.
- Place loaves into greased 5 x 9" (13 x 23 cm/2 L) loaf pans. Let rise in a warm place until doubled in volume.
- Bake at 350°F (180°C) for 20 to 25 minutes, or until bottom of loaves are browned and sound hollow when tapped.

NOTE   Rye flour contains less gluten than all-purpose or bread flour, therefore, rye bread will not rise well without additional gluten.

YIELD   **2 LOAVES**

MULTI-GRAIN & SUNFLOWER SEED BREAD

GREAT TEXTURE MEANS HIGH FIBER

3 cups	all-purpose flour	750 mL
½ cup	quick-cooking oat flakes	125 mL
2 tbsp.	raw sunflower seeds	30 mL
3 cups	warm water	750 mL
2 tbsp.	liquid honey	30 mL
2 tsp.	salt	10 mL
2 tbsp.	butter	30 mL
2 tbsp.	instant yeast	30 mL
1 cup	dark rye flour	250 mL
2-3 cups	whole-wheat bread flour	500-750 mL
	vegetable oil	

- In an electric mixer, with a dough hook, combine 3 cups (750 mL) flour, oat flakes, sunflower seeds, water, honey, salt and butter. Mix in yeast.
- Gradually add remaining flour until dough comes away from the sides of the bowl. Knead for 8-9 minutes, or until dough is smooth and pliable.
- Turn dough out onto an oiled surface, divide into 3 portions and form loaves. Place loaves into greased 5 x 9" (13 x 23 cm/2 L) loaf pans. Let rise in a warm place until doubled in volume.
- Bake at 375°F (190°C) for 20-25 minutes, or until bottoms of loaves are browned and sound hollow when tapped.

YIELD   **3 LOAVES**

Very high in polyunsaturated fat and low in saturated fat, sunflower seeds and oil have been used by Native americans for over 5,000 years. An excellent source of the antioxidant vitamin E, which has major anti-inflammatory effects, sunflower seeds are also a good source of magnesium and selenium. With their high fat content, shelled sunflower seeds should be stored in the refrigerator or freezer in airtight containers. Sunflower seeds may be added to salads, sandwiches and breads or enjoyed as a snack.

CHEESE BREAD/BUNS

BE CREATIVE – TRY A VARIETY OF INTERESTING SHAPES WITH
THIS TASTY BASIC CHEESE DOUGH RECIPE

½ cup	warm water	125 mL
½ tsp.	sugar	2 mL
1 tbsp.	yeast (1 envelope, 7 g)	15 mL
2 cups	warm water	500 mL
¼ cup	sugar	60 mL
1½ tsp.	salt	7 mL
2	eggs, beaten	2
¼ cup	oil	60 mL
6 cups	all-purpose flour	1.5 L
2 cups	grated Cheddar cheese	500 mL

- Place ½ cup (125 mL) of warm water in a small bowl. Stir in ½ tsp. (2 mL) sugar. Sprinkle yeast on top of water. Set aside for 10 minutes.
- Pour 2 cups (500 mL) of warm water into a large mixing bowl; add ¼ cup (60 mL) sugar, salt, eggs and oil. Mix well. Add the yeast mixture. Mix well.
- Add 2 cups (500 mL) of flour and beat until smooth.
- Combine 1 cup (250 mL) of flour with the grated cheese. Add to the batter. Mix well.
- Gradually add the remaining 3 cups (750 mL) of flour. Work in flour with a wooden spoon or with your hands as the dough stiffens. Place dough on a floured surface and knead until it is smooth and elastic.
- Place dough in a greased bowl. Cover and let rise in a warm place until double in size, about 1 hour. Punch down and let rise again until double in size. Punch down and let dough rest for 15 minutes. Form into buns or bread as desired. Let rise until double in size.
- Bake at 375°F (190°C) until golden brown. The baking time depends on the size of pans used. Regular loaves take 30-40 minutes; smaller loaves or buns take 15-20 minutes to bake.

VARIATION To shape loaves into **Kolach**, a braided ring-shaped bread, take ⅓ of dough; divide into 9 equal pieces. Roll 2 pieces in a cylindrical shape to 8" (20 cm). Place the 2 lengths side by side. Starting from the centre, twine dough from left to right to form a rope-like twist. Position the twisted dough into a circle, leaving a small space in the centre. Cut the ends at an angle and join together by pinching. Take a third piece of dough and roll into a cylindrical shape long enough to enclose the twined circle. Repeat with the remaining dough.

YIELD **3 LOAVES**

DILLY CHEESE BREAD

FRESH FRAGRANT DILL ADDS WONDERFUL FLAVOR

2 cups	2% creamed cottage cheese	500 mL
1 cup	warm water	250 mL
2 tbsp.	vegetable oil	30 mL
2 tbsp.	sugar	30 mL
2 tbsp.	dried, chopped onion flakes	30 mL
2 tsp.	salt	10 mL
2	eggs, beaten	2
2 tbsp.	chopped, fresh dillweed	30 mL
2 cups	all-purpose flour	500 mL
2 tbsp.	instant yeast	30 mL
3-4 cups	all-purpose flour	750 mL-1 L

- Heat the cottage cheese to lukewarm.
- In an electric mixer, with a dough hook, briefly mix cottage cheese, water, oil, sugar, onion, salt, eggs, dillweed and 2 cups (500 mL) flour.
- While continuing to mix, sprinkle with yeast. Add remaining flour until dough comes away from the sides of the bowl.
- Knead dough for 5-6 minutes, or until smooth and elastic.
- Transfer dough to a lightly greased bowl. Cover with plastic wrap and let rise until doubled in volume.
- Transfer dough to a lightly oiled work surface. Divide dough into 3 portions and form loaves.
- Place loaves into greased 5 x 9" (13 x 23 cm/2 L) bread pans. Cover and let rise again until doubled.
- Bake at 350°F (180°C) for 30 minutes, or until golden brown. Remove loaves from pans and cool on a wire rack.

YIELD   3 LOAVES

KALAMATA OLIVE BREAD

A CRUSTY, DENSE LOAF — DIP INTO OLIVE OIL AND BALSAMIC VINEGAR OR SERVE
WITH BRUSCHETTA MIXTURE OR TAPENADE — HEAVENLY

1 cup	whole milk	250 mL
2 tsp.	butter	10 mL
2 tsp.	sugar	10 mL
1 cup	water, room temperature	250 mL
2 tsp.	instant yeast	10 mL
¾-1 cup	sliced, pitted kalamata olives	175-250 mL
1-2 tsp.	chopped capers OR fresh thyme	5-10 mL
1½ tsp.	salt	7 mL
4½ cups	all-purpose flour	1.125 L
	olive oil	
1	egg white, slightly beaten	1

- In small saucepan, bring milk to simmer; add butter and sugar. Pour into large bowl. Add water and cool until lukewarm, about 10 minutes.
- Stir in yeast. Stir in olives, thyme and salt.
- Stir in 1 cup (250 mL) flour until incorporated. Add 3 cups (750 mL) flour, 1 cup (250 mL) at a time, stirring vigorously. If necessary, add up to ½ cup (125 mL) more flour, until dough is smooth and pulls away from sides of bowl.
- Oil large bowl. Transfer dough to bowl; turn to coat with oil. Cover bowl with plastic wrap. Let dough rise until doubled, about 45 minutes (do NOT punch down).
- Turn dough out onto floured work surface, (do NOT punch down or knead). Divide dough into 2 pieces. Gently form (do NOT knead) each piece into 15 x 2¼" (38 x 6 cm) loaves (dough will be rough in texture). Place loaves on oiled baking sheet. Cover loosely with plastic wrap. Let rise in warm place until slightly puffed, about 15 minutes.
- Brush tops of loaves with beaten egg white. For crusty loaves, spritz inside of oven with water. Bake loaves at 500°F (260°C) for 10 minutes. Reduce oven temperature to 400°F (200°C) and bake for 25-30 minutes, until loaves are browned and sound hollow when tapped. Cool on rack.

YIELD   2 SMALL LOAVES

FOCACCIA

FLAVORFUL TOPPINGS CROWN THIS DELICIOUS ITALIAN FLATBREAD

1¼ cups	milk, scalded	300 mL
¼ cup	sugar	60 mL
2 tsp.	salt	10 mL
⅓ cup	olive oil	75 mL
1 tsp.	sugar	5 mL
½ cup	warm water	125 mL
1 tbsp.	active dry yeast (1 envelope)	15 mL
1	egg	1
3-3½ cups	all-purpose flour	750-875 mL
1 tbsp.	EACH onion & garlic powders	15 mL
1 tbsp.	dry Italian seasoning	15 mL
	olive oil	
	additional dry Italian seasoning	
	coarse salt	

- In a large bowl, combine milk, sugar, salt and olive oil. Let cool.
- Dissolve 1 tsp. (5 mL) sugar in warm water. Sprinkle yeast over water and let sit for 10 minutes.
- Beat egg into milk mixture. Add 1 cup (250 mL) of flour; beat on high speed until well blended. Add yeast mixture; beat for 2 minutes. Add 1 cup (250 mL) of flour; beat for 5 minutes, or until smooth.
- In a small bowl, combine the third cup of flour with onion and garlic powders and Italian seasoning. Mix into dough until blended and smooth. Knead in some or all of the remaining ½ cup (125 mL) of flour, only until the dough is smooth and elastic.
- Cover bowl with plastic wrap and a tea towel; let rise in a warm place until doubled in volume. With oiled fingers, spread dough in a well-greased 12 x 12" (30 x 30 cm) baking pan. Let rise for 1 hour.
- Brush with olive oil. Sprinkle with Italian seasoning and coarse salt.
- Bake at 400°F (200°C) for 15-20 minutes, or until golden brown.
- Serve warm or cool.

VARIATION   For a ***Kalamata Olive Focaccia***, add 3-4 tbsp. (45-60 mL) chopped kalamata olives to dough with the seasonings.

YIELD   *1 LOAF*

BRAIDED SESAME LOAF

DECORATIVE BRAIDED LOAVES ARE A CHERISHED EUROPEAN TRADITION

1 cup	milk	250 mL
¼ cup	butter	60 mL
1 tbsp.	sugar	15 mL
2 cups	all-purpose flour	500 mL
1½ tsp.	salt	7 mL
2	eggs, beaten	2
2 tsp.	instant yeast	10 mL
1½-2 cups	all-purpose flour	375-500 mL
1 tbsp.	milk	15 mL
2 tbsp.	sesame seeds	30 mL

- Gently heat milk, butter and sugar to melt butter and dissolve sugar.
- In a large bowl, combine milk mixture, 2 cups (500 mL) of flour and salt.
- Set aside 1 tbsp. (15 mL) of beaten egg; add remainder to batter.
- Sprinkle yeast over batter; stir in. Add remaining flour until a soft dough forms. Knead until smooth and elastic.
- Place dough in a greased bowl; cover with plastic wrap and let rise in a warm place until doubled in volume.
- Knead dough for about 2 minutes. Divide into 3 equal pieces. Shape each piece into a rope shape about 10" (25 cm) long.
- Lay dough pieces lengthwise on a greased 10 x 15" (25 x 38 cm) baking pan. Braid dough, pinching ends to seal. Cover with plastic wrap; let rise until doubled in volume.
- Whisk milk into reserved 1 tbsp. (15 mL) of beaten egg. Brush over braid. Sprinkle with sesame seeds.
- Bake at 350°F (180°C) for 20 to 25 minutes, or until golden brown and hollow sounding when tapped on the bottom.

YIELD   1 LARGE BRAIDED LOAF

INDEX

CENTAX COOKBOOKS MAKE GREAT GIFTS

All the Tea in China _____	x $7.95 =	$_____
Flavors of Home _____	x $19.95 =	$_____
Grandma's Best _____	x $21.95 =	$_____
Grandma's Kitchen _____	x $21.95 =	$_____
Grandma's Soups & Salads _____	x $21.95 =	$_____
Grandma's Touch _____	x $21.95 =	$_____
201 Fat-Burning Recipes _____	x $19.95 =	$_____
Create Your Own – Bride's Cookbook _____	x $12.95 =	$_____
Create Your Own – College Survival Recipes _____	x $12.95 =	$_____
Create Your Own – Grilled Cheese Cookbook _____	x $12.95 =	$_____
Create Your Own – Holiday Cookbook _____	x $12.95 =	$_____
Create Your Own – Recipes By Me Cookbook _____	x $12.95 =	$_____
Shipping and handling charge (total order) _____	=	$ 4.00
Subtotal _____	=	$_____
In Canada add 7% GST _____	=	$_____
Total enclosed _____	=	$_____

U.S. and international orders payable in U.S. funds/Prices subject to change.

NAME: _____

STREET: _____

CITY: _____ PROV./STATE _____

COUNTRY: _____ POSTAL CODE/ZIP: _____

❑ CHEQUE **OR** Charge to ❑ VISA ❑ MASTERCARD

Account Number: ☐☐☐☐☐☐☐☐☐☐☐☐☐☐☐☐

Expiry Date: ☐☐☐☐

Telephone (in case we have a question about your order): _____

Make cheque or money order payable
TO: **Centax Books & Distribution** **OR** Order by phone, fax or email:
    1150 Eighth Avenue   **Phone: 1-800-667-5595**
    Regina, Saskatchewan   **FAX: 1-800-823-6829**
    Canada   S4R 1C9   **E-mail: centax@printwest.com**

**See our website for our complete range of cookbooks,
gardening books, history books, etc.
www.centaxbooks.com**

For fund-raising or volume purchases, contact Centax Books & Distribution
for volume rates. Please allow 2-3 weeks for delivery.

CENTAX COOKBOOKS MAKE GREAT GIFTS

ALL THE TEA IN CHINA – Fascinating Traditions & Incredible Edibles
by Yvonne Wrightman

Tea history, traditions and customs from around the world are complemented by recipes for delectable scones, sandwiches, savories, pastries, tarts, cakes and Indian Tea Treats. From the elegant rituals of afternoon tea, to cosy, casual high tea suppers, or the friendly "cuppa" around the kitchen table, a steaming cup of tea revives both body and spirit. *All The Tea in China* is a lovely blend of delicious flavors and intriguing information.

Retail $7.95	6" x 9"
64 pages	12 line drawings
ISBN 1-895292-35-2	saddle stitched binding

GRANDMA'S KITCHEN – Traditional Comfort Cooking – over 400,000 sold in series
by Irene Hrechuk and Verna Zasada

Remembering grandma's kitchen always conjures up images of comforting aromas and satisfying flavors. Grandma's kitchens contain memories of some of the best food the world has to offer, from generations of great home cooks. With this cookbook you can prepare your special childhood favorites as grandma used to make them. You can also prepare some of the fabulous recipes made by your friends' grandmas.

Retail $21.95	7" x 10"
208 pages	10 colour photographs
ISBN 1-894022-86-6	perfect bound

FLAVORS OF HOME – Creative Home Cooking
by Patti Shenfield

Back in Print! Tempting homestyle recipes feature imaginative variations to delight all cooks. Variations encourage novice cooks to be creative and offer enticing flavor variety. Basic crêpes range from sweet to savory options. A basic sourdough recipe includes cheese muffins, French loaf and other options. Soup, salad and dessert recipes all emphasize the adaptability of good basic recipes. This is creative comfort food with flavor and flair.

Retail $19.95	7" x 10"
208 pages	10 colour photographs
ISBN 1-894022-68-8	perfect bound

GRANDMA'S TOUCH – Tasty, Traditional & Tempting – over 400,000 sold in series
by Irene Hrechuk and Verna Zasada

Enjoy your special childhood favorites as Grandma used to make them, updated for today's busy, health-conscious cooks. Enjoy your favorite comfort food from your British, Chinese, French, German, Italian, Irish, Mexican, Russian, Scandinavian and Ukrainian grandmothers. These recipes, using readily available ingredients, are economical, easy to prepare and will delight beginner and experienced cooks.

Retail $21.95	7" x 10"
208 pages	10 colour photographs
ISBN 0-919845-79-7	perfect bound

GRANDMA'S BEST – Traditional Treats – over 400,000 sold in series
by Irene Hrechuk and Verna Zasada

Grandma's Best represents the rich multicultural aspect of our lives and includes treasured family recipes from many cultural groups. A special children's section has recipes that children love and love to make. This satisfying collection of grandma's favorite recipes will please everyone from grandkids to grandads. Here are the satisfying, comforting aromas and flavors that you remember from Grandma's kitchen.

Retail $21.95	7" x 10"
208 pages	10 colour photographs
ISBN 1-894022-66-1	perfect bound

201 FAT-BURNING RECIPES
by Cathi Graham

Master your metabolism. Cathi Graham lost 186 pounds and has kept it off for over 10 years without dieting. This book complements her Fresh Start™ program. Although there were no foods she wouldn't allow herself, she ate a high-calorie intake of proven "fat-burning" foods. These easy recipes feature fibre-rich or high-carbohydrate/low-fat foods. Calorie and fat counts are included. Here are great recipes for losing weight or just for maintaining a healthy lifestyle.

Retail $19.95	5¾" x 8½"
248 pages	5 colour photographs
ISBN 1-895292-34-4	perfect bound

CREATE YOUR OWN COOKBOOKS

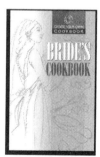

BRIDE'S COOKBOOK
ISBN 1-894022-46-7

MY HOLIDAY RECIPES & TRADITIONS
ISBN 1-894022-55-6

RECIPES BETTER THAN A GRILLED CHEESE SANDWICH –
for Students & Singles
ISBN 1-894022-45-9

RECIPES BY ME & OTHER SPECIAL PEOPLE
ISBN 1-894022-44-0

MY COLLEGE SURVIVAL RECIPES
ISBN 1-894022-93-9

Create Your Own Cookbooks – each includes a roasting chart, herb and spice chart, ingredient substitutions, ingredient equivalent measures, metric conversion tables, kitchen tips and household hints.

EACH *Create Your Own Cookbook* RETAILS FOR $12.95, 6" x 9", has **144 pages**
with illustrations throughout and lay-flat coil binding.